THE Economy COOK BOOK

ACKNOWLEDGEMENTS

The author and publisher wish to express their
gratitude to the following for their cooperation
in the production of this book:

British Bacon Curers' Association
British Farm Produce Council
British Meat Service
British Poultry Information Service
British Sausage Bureau
Pasta Information Centre
White Fish Authority
White Fish Kitchen
National Federation of Meat Traders' Associations

THE Economy COOK BOOK

MARY GRIFFITHS
OF THE
DAILY MIRROR

David & Charles
Newton Abbot – London – Vancouver

British Library Cataloguing in Publication Data

Griffiths, Mary
    Economy cook book.
    1. Cookery
    I. Title
    641.5'52   TX652
    ISBN 0–7153–7542–3

Illustrations: John Allard

First published by Mirror Books Ltd 1975
This David & Charles edition 1978

© Mirror Books Ltd 1975

Printed in Great Britain
by A. Wheaton & Co Ltd, Exeter
for David & Charles (Publishers) Limited
Brunel House Newton Abbot Devon

Published in Canada
by Douglas David & Charles Limited
1875 Welch Street North Vancouver BC

CONTENTS

INTRODUCTION

If you are a "take six eggs" type of cook, don't read on!

This is an economy cook book aimed at providing a family meal as cheaply as is reasonably possible. By that I mean cheaply cooked and with cheaper ingredients.

To save food costs the best advice is to remember the Economy Cooks' Rules:

- Cook seasonally
- Buy cheaply
- And don't waste!

That means cook the vegetables currently in season; buy the fore-quarters or "special offers" in meat (or fish) and buy only the quantities your family need.

Because the emphasis throughout the following 100-plus recipes is on economy I have cut out the use of many herbs and spices. They do improve the flavour of many dishes but I don't want inexperienced cooks to be blinded by cookery science and prevented from trying a recipe because it uses herbs they don't know!

To save cash in the kitchen, here are a few more money-saving notions:

- Foil can be wiped clean on a kitchen work surface with a dish cloth – and re-used.
- Peel root vegetables thinly. Otherwise you are throwing food value – and money – into the waste bin.
- Cultivated mushrooms don't need peeling. Just rinse in cold water and wipe.
- If you pour boiling water over cooking apples immediately before peeling, they can be peeled very thinly.
- The dark green, tough leaves of cabbage, the pale greenery on celery, the coarser leaves of lettuce, the stump of a cauliflower – they all have something to offer, too. Chop them up and put them into a thick vegetable soup or add them to a stew.

One further tip: Read the recipe through carefully before you begin.

MEAT

Meat costs money. That is an evident fact! But the cheapest cuts of meat provide the same nourishment and goodness as the most expensive.

Since this book is concerned with economy, perhaps the best advice you can have is that you don't need prime cuts to get good food and tasty meals.

There are tricks to "stretch" the meat in a dish – and, as always, to keep prices down, cook in season.

All meat should be placed in a refrigerator on a plate and covered lightly to prevent it drying out.

It's best cooked within two to three days and, ideally, it should be removed from the refrigerator an hour before cooking to let it reach room temperature and full flavour.

Don't buy too much and then find yourself with waste. With meat – that is a very expensive practice.

Amounts to buy per person:

Frying or grilling steak	5 – 6 oz.
Roasting meat – with bone	8 oz.
Roasting meat – without bone	5 – 6 oz.
Mince meat	4 – 5 oz.
Stewing meat with bone	6 – 8 oz.
Stewing meat without bone	4 – 5 oz.

(As a guide, you need about half a pint of gravy for four servings.)

When costing a meat meal – work it out at the cost-per-serving, not just the cost-per-lb. Boneless meat may appear more expensive than the same meat on-the-bone, but there will be virtually no waste off the bone.

BEEF

The cheaper cuts normally require longer, slower cooking.

Know what you are buying. Here are some economical cuts and their uses.

Top Rump Lean cut usually sold sliced ready for frying or braising. As a joint, requires slow, moist cooking, such as pot-roasting.

Brisket Sold on the bone or boned and rolled. Needs slow, moist cooking. Often salted or pickled for pressed beef.

Silverside Traditional for boiled beef and carrots. Also sold pickled ready for boiling.

Shin and Leg Excellent soup meats. Cook on bone to give jelly stock. Invaluable for soups, stews and casseroles.

Neck and Clod Full flavour for hot-pots and stews.

Flank For pot-roasting on the bone and also for stews and hot-pots.

Chuck and Blade Ideal for braising, stewing, puddings and pies.

Skirt Tasty and economical for stewing.

If a recipe calls for stock – use a meat cube in an emergency!

To choose good quality beef, look for meat which is firm, with a good red bloom. The lean should be speckled with fat, known as "marbling", and the prime cuts should be free of gristle.

BEEF

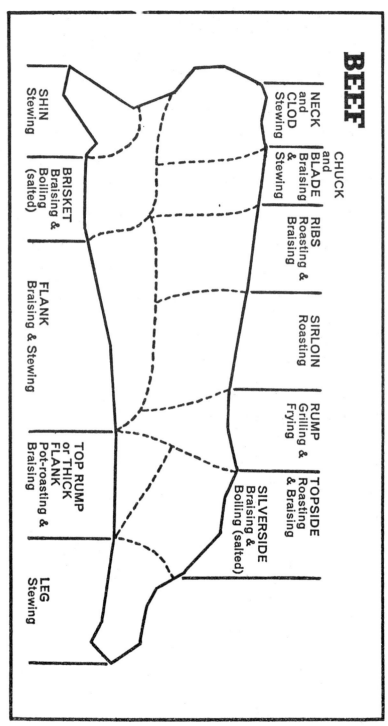

SHIN
Stewing

NECK
and
CLOD
Stewing

CHUCK
and
BLADE
Braising
&
Stewing

RIBS
Roasting &
Braising

SIRLOIN
Roasting

RUMP
Grilling &
Frying

TOPSIDE
Roasting
& Braising

SILVERSIDE
Braising &
Boiling (salted)

LEG
Stewing

BRISKET
Braising &
Boiling
(salted)

FLANK
Braising & Stewing

TOP RUMP
or THICK
FLANK
Pot-roasting &
Braising

This can be cooked on top of the stove in one dish when you need something cheap midweek.

MIDWEEK SPECIAL

Serves 4   Cooking time 1½ hours

YOU NEED:
1½ lb top rump or stewing beef
1 oz lard
1 sliced onion
½ lb of any mixed sliced vegetables
½ pint stock
Seasoning

METHOD:
1 Cut the meat into 4 slices (or ask the butcher if he will do so) and fry it in the lard in a large saucepan with a lid, until browned.
2 Remove the meat from the pan while you fry the onion and mixed vegetables in the juices for about 4–5 minutes.
3 Replace the meat in the pan, add the stock, and season as you like.
4 Cover the pan with the lid and cook very slowly for about 1½ hours.
  The gravy can be thickened before serving if desired.

When green peppers are cheap – try this. Peppers, incidentally, are absolutely not hot.

PEPPER BEEF CASSEROLE

Serves 6   Cooking time 2½ hours

YOU NEED:
2 lb cubed chuck steak
2 tablespoons seasoned flour
1 oz dripping
2 sliced onions
1 blanched and sliced green pepper
15-oz can of tomatoes
¾ pint stock
Pinch of paprika pepper (if it's handy)

METHOD:
1 Toss the meat in the flour you have already seasoned with salt and pepper.
2 Melt the dripping in a flameproof casserole and lightly fry the steak, adding the sliced onion for a minute or two.
3 Add the paprika if you are using it – otherwise use ordinary pepper.
4 Continue frying until everything is nicely browned before adding the sliced green pepper (previously blanched by dropping in boiling water for a minute or two).
5 Tip in the tomatoes and stock, and stir to mix evenly.
6 Cover tightly and cook in the oven for about 2½ hours at 350° or Mark 4.

This is a simplified Belgian dish – cooked on top of the stove which is cheaper than in the oven.

CARBONADE OF BEEF

Serves 6   **Cooking time 2 hours**

YOU NEED:
2 lb of cubed chuck steak
1½ oz butter
1 large sliced onion
1 teaspoon salt
¾ pint stock (or beer would be lovely)
2 teaspoons French mustard
2 teaspoons brown sugar
2 teaspoons vinegar
2 ozs white breadcrumbs
1 bay leaf and a pinch of thyme will add flavour

METHOD:
1 Fry the onion in the butter in a heavy based saucepan.
2 Add the beef and fry until browned.
3 Now stir in all the remaining ingredients except the bread-crumbs.
4 Bring to the boil – cover firmly and reduce to a simmer for about 2 hours. Stir in the breadcrumbs, remove the bay leaf – and serve with boiled potatoes.

The Dutch make minced beef go a long way like this.

DUTCH MEAT BALLS

Serves 4   Cooking time 30 minutes

YOU NEED:
1 lb mince
1 beaten egg
1 grated onion
2 oz breadcrumbs
3 tablespoons oil
1 sliced onion
4 oz sliced mushrooms
1 tablespoon flour
1 tablespoon tomato purée
$\frac{1}{2}$ pint stock
2 oz cooked noodles
Seasoning

METHOD:
1 Mix the first 3 ingredients together with 1 oz breadcrumbs, season well and form into 12 balls. Roll these in the breadcrumbs you've got left.
2 Heat the oil and fry the meatballs for about 15 minutes, by which time they should be crisp all over. Remove and keep them warm in a casserole dish.
3 Fry the sliced onion in the juices remaining in the pan until tender and add the mushrooms. Cook for another 2–3 minutes.
4 Remove this mixture from the pan and add it to the casserole dish.
5 Stir the flour into the remaining oil in the pan and cook for 2–3 minutes.
6 Gradually pour in the stock and the tomato purée and boil up before adding to the casserole too.
7 Cover the casserole and cook in the oven for about 30 minutes at 350° or Mark 4.
8 Before serving, add the cooked noodles and you've a complete meal.

Apples make an unusual addition to beef stew – and are a cheap way of stretching it.

BEEF & APPLE STEW

Serves 4   Cooking time 2½ hours

YOU NEED:
1½ lb cubed shin of beef
1 oz flour (seasoned with a teaspoon each of dry mustard
  and mixed herbs)
2 oz dripping
2 sliced onions
2 sliced carrots
4 oz sliced mushrooms
2 tablespoons vinegar
¾ pint stock
1 large cooking apple (peeled, cored and thinly sliced)

METHOD:
1 Toss the meat in the flour and fry in the hot dripping in a flameproof casserole.
2 Remove the meat and fry the onions and carrots until golden brown.
3 Remove these and spoon the vinegar into the oil remaining in the casserole.
4 Boil until most of the vinegar has evaporated.
5 Add the stock and put the meat and vegetables, with the mushrooms, back into the casserole.
6 Cover and cook in the oven for about 2 hours at 325° or Mark 3.
7 Add the apples and cook for another 30 minutes.

This recipe makes a little mince go a long, long way.

GOLDEN BURGERS

Serves 4   Cooking time 10 minutes

YOU NEED:
1 large grated potato
8 oz minced beef
1 chopped onion
1 teaspoon brown sauce
1 dessertspoon chopped parsley
4 oz flour
1 egg
$\frac{1}{4}$ pint milk
Fat for frying
Pinch of mixed herbs (optional)

METHOD:
1 Tip the potato, beef, onion, sauce, parsley and herbs (if you are using them), into a bowl and mix thoroughly.
2 Take the mixture out and form into four rounds.
3 Put the flour in the bowl with a little salt and the egg, and gradually beat the whole lot up with the milk to form a thickish batter.
4 Dip the burgers in this and then fry until golden in hot fat or oil (about 5 minutes each side on a low heat. Anything less and the meat and potatoes won't be cooked!)
Serve with anything you fancy – but a salad is nice.

Using onions for stuffing makes this a really economical dish.

BRAISED STUFFED BRISKET

Serves 6–8   Cooking time 2¼ hours

YOU NEED:
3 lb rolled brisket
3 chopped bacon rashers
4 large onions
½ oz breadcrumbs
1 oz dripping
1 oz butter
Seasoning

METHOD:
1 Peel the onions and boil them for 8–10 minutes to soften them.
2 Carefully take out the cores with a spoon. Mix the cores with the chopped bacon, breadcrumbs and butter, seasoning well – and refill the onion centres.
3 The stuffing you've got left over has a place too … push it into the spaces in the roll of brisket. Make sure it's still well tied and brown it all over in hot dripping in a frying pan.
4 Take it out and wrap it in *double* foil, sealing firmly.
5 Put this parcel into a dry tin (no fat) and cook in the centre of the oven for 1½ hours at 450° or Mark 8.
6 Now open the oven and put the stuffed onions on the bottom shelf and cook everything for about 40 minutes more.
    The juices that collect in the foil will make a nice gravy to go on top of the onions.

A simple pie warms a winter day!

STEAK & ONION PIE

Serves 6   Cooking time 30 minutes

YOU NEED:
1½ lb cubed skirt
1 tablespoon flour
2 oz dripping
2 sliced onions
4 oz sliced mushrooms
½ pint stock
½ lb puff pastry (buy it)

METHOD:
1 Coat the meat in flour and fry in the hot dripping in a 2-pint flameproof dish until it is brown.
2 Add the onions and fry for 2–3 minutes, then add the mushrooms and fry those for a minute or so.
3 Add the stock, cover the dish and simmer for about 1½ hours. Leave to cool.
4 Add enough liquid to come halfway up the dish.
5 Cover the top with the pastry, sealing the edges firmly and brush the top with milk to brown nicely.
6 Bake in the oven about 30 minutes at 425° or Mark **7.**

LAMB

From May to October home-produced lamb is usually plentiful – but imported lamb, mainly from New Zealand, is readily available for the rest of the year.

Broadly speaking, chops and legs are better bargains in winter and early spring.

When buying lamb, look for a fine-grained appearance, moist and pink flesh and firm, white fat.

Leg and shoulders should be plump with a bluish tinge on the knuckles and a paper-thin layer of skin covering the meat.

The economical cuts are:

Shoulder An economical roast whether on the bone, or boned, stuffed and rolled. Makes rich and tasty casseroles. Often divided into two smaller cuts – blade end and knuckle end. Both are good for roasting or braising.

Best end Neck Reliable roast on the bone, or boned, stuffed and rolled. Often sold as cutlets for grilling or frying.

Middle Neck Usually cut into chops for casseroles. The basis of the famous Lancashire Hot-pot.

Breast Most economical cut for roasting or braising. Makes tasty casseroles.

Scrag Very economical for soups and stews.

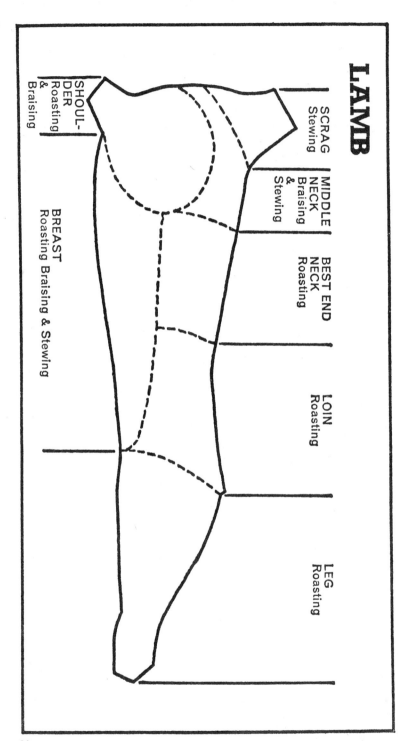

LAMB

SCRAG
Stewing

MIDDLE
NECK
Braising
&
Stewing

BEST END
NECK
Roasting

LOIN
Roasting

LEG
Roasting

SHOUL-
DER
Roasting
&
Braising

BREAST
Roasting Braising & Stewing

You can get a really cheap meal out of a best end neck of lamb, boned and rolled by the butcher.

NOISETTES OF LAMB—& ONION SAUCE

Serves 4   Cooking time 20 minutes

YOU NEED:
1 boned and rolled best end of neck
1 packet of onion sauce

METHOD:
1 Make sure the lamb is securely tied with string at 1" intervals.
2 Slice in between the string – and you've got what are called "noisettes" of lamb.
3 Grill these for about 6–8 minutes each side, during which time make up the onion sauce as the packet directs.
4 You can, if you wish, shred a small carrot into the sauce as it is cooking to give it extra colour.
5 Serve the lamb with the sauce separately and perhaps peas and tomatoes. Simple!

BARBECUED LAMB

Serves 4   Cooking time 10 minutes

YOU NEED:
12 oz cold lamb slices
$1\frac{1}{2}$ oz melted butter
3 teaspoons vinegar
4 tablespoons redcurrant jelly
$\frac{1}{4}$ pint stock
A little dry mustard
Seasoning

METHOD:
1 Make a "piquant" sauce by melting the butter in a frying pan and adding everything else but the lamb.
2 When nicely blended – add the lamb and heat through.
3 Serve with the sauce and fresh vegetables.

This is an English version of Greek Kebabs.

KEBABS & NOODLES

Serves 4   **Cooking time 20 minutes**

YOU NEED:
$\frac{3}{4}$ lb fillet neck of lamb
2 tablespoons vinegar
4 tablespoons oil
$\frac{1}{2}$ tablespoon chopped parsley
Seasoning
2 oz mushrooms
3 small onions
3 firm tomatoes
6 oz ribbon noodles

METHOD:
1 Mix together the vinegar, oil, parsley and plenty of salt and pepper.
2 Cut the lamb into cubes and leave it to marinate (or "soak") in the mixture for a couple of hours, or overnight in the fridge.
3 Peel the onions and boil for about 2 minutes. Drain and cut into quarters.
4 Heat the grill when you are ready to eat and thread the meat, mushrooms, tomato and onion alternately on to four meat skewers.
5 Lay these on the grill rack and brush with the marinade.
6 Grill the kebabs for 10–15 minutes, turning once and basting with the marinade.
7 Cook the noodles in boiling, salted water for about 10 minutes.
8 Drain and rinse, and then return to the pan to warm while a knob of butter melts on top.

Shoulder is good – but a bit awkward to cut. So buy it boned, and cook it like this.

STUFFED LAMB IN THE ROUND

Serves 6   Cooking time approx. 1 hour (see recipe)

YOU NEED:
1 boned shoulder
2–3 chopped onions
2 tablespoons chopped parsley
1 oz melted butter

METHOD:
1 Mix the onions and parsley and stuff the meat in the pocket left by the bone.
2 Skewer firmly and tie well into a round shape.
3 Brush with melted butter and roast for 25 minutes per lb, and 25 minutes over, at 350° or Mark 4 (if you like it "pink".) – 400° or Mark 6 will make it well done.
4 Remove the skewer and string before serving, of course! It will cut well into wedges.

For a special treat, try these alternative stuffings.

APRICOT STUFFING

YOU NEED:
2 oz breadcrumbs
3 oz dried, chopped apricots
1 chopped onion
3–4 tablespoons milk
Seasoning

METHOD:
Mix all the ingredients together until nicely blended – and stuff as before.

COTTAGE MINT STUFFING

YOU NEED:
4 oz breadcrumbs
1 chopped onion
1 heaped tablespoon dried or fresh, chopped mint
Juice of one lemon
Little milk to bind
Seasoning

METHOD:
Mix and use in exactly the same way as the apricot stuffing.

Here's a simple dish – a complete meal – with casseroled vegetables and stuffing.

LAMB ROLL

Serves 4–5   Cooking time $2\frac{1}{4}$ hours

YOU NEED:
1 large (or 2 small) *boned* breasts
1 lb thinly-sliced potatoes
2 sticks chopped celery
1 sliced carrot
1 teaspoon flour
$\frac{1}{4}$ pint stock

STUFFING
MIX TOGETHER:
4 chopped rashers bacon
1 large peeled, cored and chopped cooking apple
1 tablespoon brown sugar
2 tablespoons breadcrumbs
Pinch of thyme, and seasoning

METHOD:
1 Lay the lamb breast, boned side up, on a board, and spread the stuffing mixture along it.
2 Roll it up and tie it firmly at 1″ intervals.
3 Put the roll in a casserole dish with the stock and the vegetables all round it – sprinkle the flour over them, cover and cook for $1\frac{1}{2}$ hours at 375° or Mark 5.
4 Uncover and cook another 45 minutes to brown nicely. One cooking dish and a complete meal!

Sometimes a store-cupboard tin of something or other cheers up a cheap dish.

TOMATO LAMB CASSEROLE

Serves 4–5   **Cooking time 1½–2 hours**

YOU NEED:
8 middle neck chops
4 leeks or onions
2 15-oz cans of tomatoes
2 bay leaves (optional)

METHOD:
1 Just slice the well-washed leeks or onions and put into a casserole dish with all the other ingredients.
2 Cover tightly and cook in the oven for 1½–2 hours at 350° or Mark 4.
3 Remove the bay leaves and serve with mashed potatoes or rice.

Scrag makes good soups and stews – and even pies like this one.

WELSHMAN'S PIE

Serves 4   Cooking time 1½ hours

YOU NEED:
1½ lb cubed scrag
Seasoning
2 lb peeled, cored and sliced cooking apples
1 lb sliced onions
½ pint boiling water
6 oz suet crust pastry (see recipe below)

METHOD:
1 Put the meat in a pie dish with plenty of seasoning.
2 Arrange the apples and onions on top and pour over the boiling water.
3 Cover with the pastry and bake in the centre of the oven for 1½ hours at 375° or Mark 5.

SUET CRUST:

6 oz self-raising flour
1 teaspoon salt
3 oz shredded suet
¼ pint cold water

METHOD:
1 Add suet to flour and salt and mix in water with a knife until lumps form.
2 Gather mixture together lightly and knead until smooth.
3 Turn out on a floured board and shape into a ball.
4 Leave for 10 minutes before rolling out.

LAMB MOUSSAKA

Serves 4   **Cooking time 1½ hours**

YOU NEED:
12 oz minced or chopped-up cooked lamb
½ oz butter
1 chopped onion
½ teaspoon mixed herbs
15-oz can of tomatoes
1½ lb sliced potatoes
1 teaspoon gravy powder

SAUCE:
1 oz butter
1 oz flour
½ pint milk
2 oz grated Cheddar cheese
1 beaten egg

METHOD:
1 Fry the onion in the butter for 3 minutes.
2 Add the lamb, gravy powder, herbs, teaspoon of salt and a little pepper.
3 Strain the tomatoes (and save the juice).
4 Layer the meat mixture, potatoes and tomatoes in a large casserole – finishing with potatoes.
5 Sprinkle salt on top and pour that tomato juice you've so carefully saved over the lot.
6 Now make the sauce by melting the 1 oz of butter in a pan, adding the flour, and cooking for a minute.
7 Stir in the milk, gradually, bring to the boil and cook for 2 minutes, stirring all the time.
8 Remove from the heat and beat in the cheese, egg and seasoning.
9 Pour this over the casserole, cover and cook in the middle of the oven for an hour at about 375° or Mark 5.
10 To brown the top, uncover the dish and cook for another 30 minutes.

PORK

British pork is available throughout the year, and every joint of it can be roasted, but it should never be underdone.

To ensure pork is roasted right through, pre-heat the oven to 350° or Mark 4 and allow 30 minutes per lb and 30 minutes over.

All the individual cuts are suitable too for grilling or frying – and economy cuts are ideal for stews, casseroles or pies.

When choosing pork, look for firm, dry, lean flesh with creamy-white fat. Always ask the butcher to score the skin for you.

To get the crackling firm and crisp, brush the scored skin with oil or fat and sprinkle well with salt. Roast "dry" with rind uppermost, and don't baste.

The economical cuts are:

Shoulder Large roasting joint, particularly good when boned and rolled. Often divided into blade and spare rib.

Blade Economical roasting joint. Ideal meat for braising.

Spare rib Lean and economical roasting joint with little top fat and skin. Ideal meat for home-made pork pies.

Spare rib chops Excellent for grilling, frying or braising.

Hand and Spring Large joint for roasting whole. Often divided into hand and shank.

Hand Can be boned and roasted. Also pickled and boiled.

Shank Good cut for stews.

Belly Thick end makes an economical and tasty roast. All belly is excellent for boiling and serving cold. It is often sliced and sold as an economical cut for grilling or frying. Ideal for pickling.

PORK

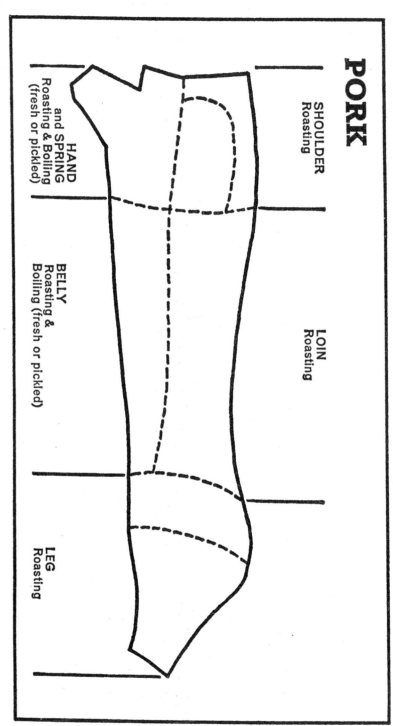

SHOULDER
Roasting

**HAND
and SPRING**
Roasting & Boiling
(fresh or pickled)

BELLY
Roasting &
Boiling (fresh or pickled)

LOIN
Roasting

LEG
Roasting

This is a colourful one-pot dish using a cheap cut of pork and seasonal vegetables. Cider tenderises - but you can use stock.

PORK BRAISE

Serves 4–5   Cooking time 1½ hours

YOU NEED:
2 lb boned hand or shoulder
2 oz lard
2 chopped onions
6 sliced tomatoes
¼ pint dry cider (or stock)

METHOD:
1 Heat the lard in a frying pan and brown the meat in it.
2 Remove the meat to a casserole dish while you fry the onions for a few minutes in the juices remaining.
3 Add the tomatoes and season.
4 Put these into the casserole with the pork, and pour the cider on top.
5 Cover with a close-fitting lid and cook in the oven for about 1½ hours at 325° or Mark 3.

Left-overs? We've got the very thing! This recipe is adapted from a Greek dish which uses vine leaves.

PORK &
CABBAGE ENVELOPE

Serves 4   Cooking time 45 minutes

YOU NEED:
8 oz minced cooked pork
½ oz butter
1 sliced onion
2 sliced carrots
2 oz long grain rice
½ pint stock (use a cube)

AND:
8 evenly-sized cabbage leaves
3 tablespoons tomato purée
½ pint boiling water

METHOD:
1 Cook the separated cabbage leaves in boiling water for just 5 minutes, and drain.
2 Fry the onion and carrot for about 3 minutes in the butter, then stir in the rice and fry that too for another minute.
3 Add the stock, bring to the boil and simmer for about 10 minutes. By then the rice should have absorbed the stock.
4 Stir in the cooked pork and season.
5 Lay out the cabbage leaves and spoon on the mixture evenly.
6 Fold up each one as neatly as you can, and place them in a shallow ovenproof dish.
7 Mix the tomato purée with the half pint of boiling water and pour over the "envelopes".
8 Cover the dish and cook in the centre of the oven for 45 minutes at 350° or Mark 4.

Cheap, quick, easy. What more could you ask?

GRILLED PORK RISOTTO

Serves 4   Cooking time 30 minutes

YOU NEED:
8 thick belly pork rashers
1 tablespoon oil
2 sliced onions
8 oz long-grain rice
$\frac{1}{4}$ lb sliced mushrooms
1$\frac{1}{2}$ pints stock
7-oz can of sweetcorn with peppers
1 level tablespoon chopped parsley

METHOD:
1 Fry the onions in the oil until nice and soft and then stir in the rice and cook for another minute.
2 Pour the stock in a little at a time – bring to the boil – and simmer for about 15 minutes.
3 Stir in the mushrooms and drained sweetcorn and cook for another 5–10 minutes or until the rice is cooked.
4 Meanwhile – back at the range – grill the pork to a luscious crispness!
5 Stir the parsley into the risotto just before serving with the rashers.

Stuffing makes a pork roast go further – used this way, it makes slices go further too, if they are cut off the joint first.

PORK ESCALOPES

Serves 4   **Cooking time 15 minutes**

YOU NEED:
1 lb thin-sliced shoulder (or leg)
1 beaten egg
1 packet sage and onion stuffing
1 oz lard

METHOD:
1 Flatten the slices of pork out firmly with a rolling pin.
2 Coat each one with the egg, dip in the stuffing and fry in the lard until brown and tender.
3 Serve with a seasonal vegetable and a spoonful of chutney.

Almonds make an unusual accompaniment to pork.

CRUNCHY SPARE RIBS

Serves 4   **Cooking time 20 minutes**

YOU NEED:
4 spare rib chops
1 tablespoon dry mustard
1 tablespoon brown sugar
1 oz shredded almonds

METHOD:
1 First sprinkle the chops with the mustard and sugar which you have mixed together and then grill to suit your taste.
2 Sprinkle the chops again – this time with the almonds – and grill for a little longer so as to brown the nuts before serving.
   Nice, nutty, crunchy flavour.

Belly of pork makes a substantial Sunday roast if boned and scored by the butcher, and stuffed like this.

STUFFED BELLY OF PORK & SAUCE

Serves 4–6   Cooking time 2½ hours

YOU NEED:
2 lb boned belly of pork
2 oz breadcrumbs
1 oz shredded suet
1 oz sultanas
½ teaspoon mixed herbs
1 beaten egg

SAUCE:
2 oz redcurrant jelly
7½-oz can of apple purée (or use fresh apples)

METHOD:
1 You should pre-heat the oven for this one to start – at 400° or Mark 6. Trim off any excess fat you can from the meat.
2 To make the stuffing, bind together the breadcrumbs, suet, sultanas and herbs with the egg.
3 Spread this mixture over the meat. Roll it up and tie with string really firmly.
4 Wrap the roll in foil and roast for 30 minutes before lowering the temperature to 350° or Mark 5. Cook for another 1¾ hours.
5 Remove the foil and crisp up the pork by turning the oven heat up again for about 15 minutes.
6 To make the sauce, melt the redcurrant jelly and add the purée. Heat through and serve separately.

In season, try this fruit-flavoured pork.

FRUITY-STUFFED PORK

Serves 4–6   Cooking time 2 hours

YOU NEED:
2 lb boned and scored belly of pork
1 small peeled, cored and chopped cooking apple
3–4 stoned and chopped damsons
1 oz breadcrumbs
Squeeze of lemon juice
½ teaspoon sugar

METHOD:
1 You need to pre-heat the oven to 350° or Mark 4.
2 Flatten the meat as much as possible (use a rolling pin firmly).
3 Mix the fruit with the other ingredients and season.
4 Spread this fruity mixture over the meat, roll it up and tie firmly with string.
5 Roast in hot dripping for 2 hours.

BACON

You can do a whole lot more with bacon than just add eggs to it and serve it for breakfast!

It's a cheaper *meat* than most and can be used for some filling main meals in summer as well as winter.

If you start with a whole fore-end of bacon, which weighs around 15 lb with the bone in, and 12–13 lb boned, you can make some worthwhile cuts in the cost of the bacon itself.

Obviously, however, you must have the facilities to keep it, and the dishes you make with it.

The following dishes were all made from just one fore-end.

You can, however, buy whatever size or cut you feel best for your purpose, and use it for any recipe in this section.

Fore-end gives five joints which are every bit as tasty as the more expensive gammon – and you also get rashers and bargain pieces which can be used up cheaply and tastily.

The more expensive part of the fore-end is prime Collar. This can make a first-class joint for Sunday (it is boneless), or it can be rashered.

The hock can be divided into three boneless joints. The slipper hock, the middle, and the end hock. In the North of England this latter joint tends to be rashered. Finally, for just a few pence, you can buy a knuckle – which is ideal as a basis for hot or cold soups.

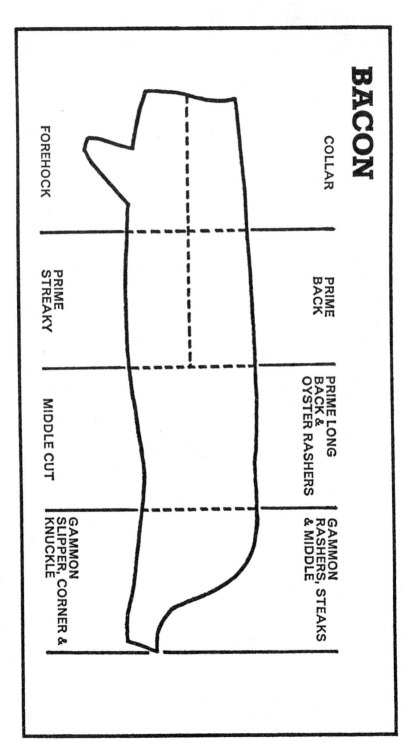

BACON

COLLAR

FOREHOCK

PRIME BACK

PRIME STREAKY

PRIME LONG BACK & OYSTER RASHERS

MIDDLE CUT

GAMMON RASHERS, STEAKS & MIDDLE

GAMMON SLIPPER, CORNER & KNUCKLE

PROVENÇAL BACON CASSEROLE

Serves 6   **Cooking time 1¼ hours**

YOU NEED:
2½–3 lb boned bacon forehock (soak it for 6 hours in cold
  water if smoked – 2 hours if unsmoked)
1½ oz dripping
2–3 onions (12 button onions would be better still!)
4 large carrots (or 12 small ones – as with onions)
4 leeks
Stock (water will do – but so would beer if you have it handy)

METHOD:
1 Put the joint in a saucepan of cold water, bring it quickly to
the boil and then simmer for 35–40 minutes.
2 Chop the vegetables.
3 Take out the joint and skin it. If you score the fat into squares
it makes it look more attractive.
4 Melt the dripping in a fireproof casserole dish and fry the
chopped vegetables for a minute or two.
5 Add the "stock" – just to cover the vegetables and put the
joint on top. If you've got a bouquet garni and some bay leaves,
you can put those in as well.
6 Cover the casserole and bake at 350° or Mark 4 for about 30
minutes more.
7 To brown, remove the lid and cook for another 10 minutes at
425° or Mark 7.
  Boiled potatoes go particularly well with this dish.

This makes a little bacon go a long way!

PAN FRIED BACON

Serves 4   Cooking time 6 minutes

YOU NEED:
4 thick collar rashers
1 egg
Packet of sage and onion stuffing
A scrap of lard

METHOD:
1 De-rind the rashers and dip into beaten egg.
2 Toss in the stuffing, and then fry in the lard for about 6 minutes until they are crisp.

For a warm summer day, try this.

CHILLED BACON SOUP

Serves 4   Cooking time 2 hours

YOU NEED:
1 knuckle of bacon
1 pig's trotter
1 onion
2 pints water
$\frac{3}{4}$ lb mixed summer vegetables (carrots, peas, beans, etc.)
1 glass of sherry (optional)

METHOD:
1 Put the knuckle and the trotter into a pan with the water.
2 Bring to the boil and simmer gently for $1\frac{1}{2}$ hours.
3 Strain and add all the vegetables, which should be diced. Cook until tender.
4 Add a glass of sherry (if you have it) and bacon cut from the bone.
5 Season and chill thoroughly.
   Very tasty served with slices of cucumber on top.

Another good summer dish – or starter course at any time is:

BACON MOUSSE

Serves 6–8

YOU NEED:
$\frac{1}{2}$ lb cooked forehock, finely minced or chopped
4 tablespoons horseradish sauce
2 tablespoons mayonnaise
$\frac{1}{2}$ teaspoon mustard powder
$\frac{1}{2}$ oz gelatine
1 tablespoon of very hot water
Top of the milk

METHOD:
1 Dissolve the gelatine in the very hot water. Allow to cool.
2 Combine with the top of the milk and mayonnaise.
3 Add the remaining ingredients, mixing thoroughly.
4 Pour into a moistened mould and chill until set.
5 Turn out and serve with hot toast – or a salad.

Want a quick T.V. supper dish for the whole family? Try this.

LIVER & BACON PÂTÉ

Serves 8   Cooking time 1½ hours

YOU NEED:
6 rashers streaky bacon
8 oz pig's liver
8 oz fat bacon
1 large onion
2 oz butter

SAUCE:
½ pint milk
2 blades mace ⎫
1 bayleaf   ⎬ if available
2–3 pepper corns ⎭
1 oz butter
1 oz flour

METHOD:
1 De-rind the streaky bacon and lay rashers at the bottom and round the sides of a greased straight-sided dish.
2 Fry liver, de-rinded fat bacon and roughly chopped onion in butter for 10 minutes.
3 Mince or put into a blender if you have one.
4 Put milk for sauce into another pan with the 2 blades of mace, 1 bayleaf and a few pepper corns if you have them.
5 Bring very slowly to the boil, leave to stand for 10 minutes, then strain.
6 Melt butter in pan, add flour and cook for 1 minute.
7 Remove from heat and gradually stir in milk.
8 Bring to the boil, stirring all the time until sauce bubbles and thickens.
9 Add to the liver mixture and blend well. Season.
10 Turn into the prepared dish and top with bay leaves. Cover with foil and a lid.
11 Stand in a roasting tin of hot water and bake for 1 hour at 350° or Mark 4.
12 Allow to become quite cold.
   Serve with toast, or salad.

CHICKEN

Chicken is first-class protein – and usually cheaper than other meat.

A plain roast chicken of about $3\frac{1}{2}$–$3\frac{3}{4}$ lb will feed four – and you need 2–3 oz of stuffing.

To cook, if it is frozen, make sure it has thawed completely, brush with oil or fat, sprinkle with salt, wrap loosely in foil and roast for 20 minutes per lb at 350° or Mark 4 – removing foil for the last 20 minutes to brown the bird.

But most of the recipes I give here use a smaller bird – because adding vegetables or other goodies "extends" the chicken. In other words – it's cheaper to feed more!

When the recipe says "stock" use a chicken cube – or use the carcass and bones of the bird boiled up for 30 minutes in a pint or so of water with seasoning added.

It is cheaper to buy a whole chicken and joint it (giving two drumsticks and two wings) than buying joints separately – and also you can use the carcass of the chicken with the breasts for another meal.

Starting with one small chicken – you can get two meals for four like this.

CHEERY CHICKEN

Serves 4   Cooking time 1¾ hours

YOU NEED:
2 thighs and 2 drumsticks
2 tablespoons oil
1 oz butter
1 sliced onion
2 tablespoons flour
4 oz sliced mushrooms
1 medium can baked beans
¾ pint of stock
Seasoning

METHOD:
1 Fry the chicken pieces in the oil and butter in an ovenproof casserole until they are golden brown.
2 Add the onion and fry that for a few minutes, then blend in the flour. (Some people take the joints out first – I don't think it matters because you've got to put them back!)
3 Season, add the stock and boil for about 3 minutes.
4 Cover the casserole and cook in the oven for about 50 minutes at 375° or Mark 5.
5 Add the mushrooms and the baked beans and cook for another 20 minutes or so.

From the carcass you've got left, strip the chicken for this!

GOUJON OF CHICKEN

Serves 4   Cooking time 10 minutes

YOU NEED:
8 oz (or more) raw chicken
1 beaten egg
1 packet parsley & thyme stuffing
Oil for frying

METHOD:
1 Cut the chicken into thin finger strips, dip each into the beaten egg and coat with the stuffing.
2 Fry in hot oil until crisp and golden.
3 Drain and serve hot with vegetables – or cold with salad.

If you start by roasting a chicken and wonder what to do with what's left, try these.

SWEETCORN CHICKEN

Serves 4   Cooking time 15-30 minutes

YOU NEED:
6 oz diced cooked chicken
1 small can sweetcorn
1 pint stock
$\frac{1}{4}$ pint milk
8 oz diced potatoes
1 diced carrot
1 chopped stick of celery

METHOD:
1 Boil the stock and milk together. Add the vegetables and season. Cook for 15 minutes.
2 Add the chicken pieces and the drained sweetcorn and heat through thoroughly.
  Good for Sunday supper, with crusty bread.

The left-over carcass will make the stock, which, with only about 4 oz of chicken bits, makes this substantial soup.

CHICKEN FARMHOUSE SOUP

Serves 6–8   **Cooking time 45 minutes**

YOU NEED:
4 oz diced chicken
1 grated carrot
1 finely-sliced onion
2 chopped sticks celery
1 oz butter
$2\frac{1}{4}$ pints of stock
$\frac{3}{4}$ pint of cider
$1\frac{1}{2}$ oz small pasta (or long-grain rice)

METHOD:
1 Fry the vegetables in the butter for 5 minutes and add the stock and the cider. Cider isn't too expensive and improves the flavour. Really!
2 Cover and simmer gently for 15–20 minutes.
3 Now add the chicken and the pasta, or rice, and simmer for another 10–20 minutes until the pasta or rice is cooked.

A boiling chicken can be used for this simply-cooked dish too.

CHICKEN & BROAD BEANS

Serves 4–6   Cooking time 1 hour

YOU NEED:
A small boiling chicken, cut into portions
1 tablespoon lemon juice
2 oz butter
2 oz flour
2 tablespoons chopped parsley
1½ lb cooked broad beans
Seasoning and a bay leaf (if you have one)

METHOD:
1 Simmer the chicken in a saucepan of water with that bayleaf, seasoning and the lemon juice for about 45 minutes – or until it's tender.
2 Drain off the liquor and reserve it, and put the chicken to keep warm.
3 Melt the butter in a pan; gradually stir in the flour and cook for a minute.
4 Stir in 1 pint of the chicken liquor – (it's best done a little at a time).
5 Boil up the sauce and season well.
6 Throw in the parsley and the beans and simmer for 2–3 minutes.
7 Pour the beans and sauce over the chicken to serve.

A 2½-lb chicken makes this substantial dish.

CHICKEN SWEET & SOUR

Serves 4   Cooking time 1¼ hours

YOU NEED:
1 chicken
1 oz dripping
4 tablespoons tomato ketchup
½ oz flour
Juice of ½ lemon
2 teaspoons sugar
¼ teaspoon black pepper
12 pickled onions
4 oz halved mushrooms
¾ pint of stock

METHOD:
1 Cut up the chicken and fry in the dripping in a flameproof dish until lightly browned all over.
2 Dollop in the ketchup and cook for another 5 minutes gently.
3 Stir in the flour, lemon juice, sugar, pepper, pickled onions and mushrooms and tip in the stock.
4 Cover and cook in the oven at 350° or Mark 4 until the chicken is tender – an hour should do it.

When marrows are in season, this makes a change.

OVEN-BAKED CHICKEN & MARROW

Serves 4   Cooking time 1 hour

YOU NEED:
4 chicken joints
2 tablespoons cooking oil
1 medium-sized marrow
1 sliced onion
Pinch of dried herbs
15-oz can of mushroom soup

METHOD:
1 Slit the marrow into boat-shaped halves and take out the seeds. Dice it up neatly.
2 Fry the chicken joints in the oil in a flameproof casserole till nicely golden.
3 Pop the diced marrow and sliced onion into the casserole and sprinkle with those herbs ... they cheer it up and flavour tastily.
4 Pour the mushroom soup over the casserole, cover and bake in the oven at 325° or Mark 3 for about an hour.

You should have everything you need for this in your store cupboard.

BAKED CHICKEN MORNAY

Serves 4   **Cooking time 30 minutes**

YOU NEED:
4 chicken joints
1 oz seasoned flour
2½ oz butter
½ pint milk
½ oz flour
4 oz crumbled cheese
½ teaspoon made mustard
2 oz breadcrumbs

METHOD:
1 Coat the joints in the flour and pop them in an ovenproof dish.
2 Dot with 2 oz of the butter and bake at 400° or Mark 6 for 20 minutes.
3 Meanwhile, heat the milk, the remaining butter and the flour together – stirring continuously – until the sauce, like the plot, thickens!
4 Stir in the cheese; season, add the mustard and simmer gently for 2–3 minutes.
5 Tip any liquor from the cooked chicken into the sauce, stir well and tip the lot back on to the chicken.
6 Sprinkle breadcrumbs over the top – and grill till crispy and brown.

SAUSAGES

Sausages have come a long way in the world since they were christened "bangers".

We eat six thousand *million* of them every year – that's 125 for each of us!

Out of every £100 the British housewife spends on food, she spends £3 on sausages – that's how popular they are!

By law pork sausages must contain 65% meat – beef sausages only 50%, which is one reason why beef sausages are cheaper than pork.

There are distinct regional preferences. In the North they like their sausages thin – and beef. In the South they prefer them thick – and pork.

Nutritionally, sausages are a good source of protein, and ounce for ounce provide more calories than beef; more iron than cod.

To cook, do *not* prick or stab them. Turn them gently in a frying pan over a low heat for 10–15 minutes, or turn under a grill on medium heat for about 20 minutes, or bake in the oven at 375° or Mark 5 for 30 minutes.

Remember to brown sausages all over – and cook them through.

You can also barbecue them on a skewer, alternating with, say, mushrooms, tomatoes and a bacon roll.

For some more ideas – read on!

How about this meal-in-a-dish for simplicity and economy? In season, use fresh broad beans.

SAUSAGE BAKE

Serves 4   **Cooking time 30 minutes**

YOU NEED:
1 lb sausages
Can of broad beans
1 sliced onion
2 oz butter
2 oz flour
$\frac{1}{4}$ pint milk
8 oz sliced tomatoes
2 oz grated cheese
Seasoning
Squeeze of lemon juice (if it's handy)

METHOD:
1 Fry the onion in the butter until it's softened.
2 Stir in the flour.
3 Blend in the milk and the liquor from the can of beans.
4 Season, add the lemon juice (it sharpens the taste) and simmer for 5 minutes.
5 Meanwhile, brown the sausages to your own liking, grease a shallow ovenproof dish and cover the base with sliced tomatoes.
6 Tip the beans on to the tomatoes and arrange the sausages on top.
7 Pour the onion sauce over the lot and dot with the cheese.
8 Bake for 20–30 minutes at 400° or Mark 6 until the top is crisp, brown and bubbly.

To save time and effort, you could use a packet of onion sauce if you like.

Hard-boiled eggs and sausagemeat can make an interesting pie.

GYPSY PIE

Serves 4   Cooking time 45 minutes

YOU NEED:
1 lb sausagemeat
½ lb puff pastry
2 hard-boiled sliced eggs
1 tablespoon onion
½ level teaspoon sage (if you have it)
Beaten egg (or milk) to glaze

METHOD:
1 Roll out the pastry to an oblong 12″ × 14″. Cut off a piece 12″ × 6″ and place on a wetted baking sheet. (This is only so you'll be able to lift it off!)
2 Spread half the sausagemeat over this pastry, leaving a 1″ margin all round.
3 Lay the eggs over the sausagemeat, sprinkle with the onions, salt and pepper, and sage.
4 Cover carefully with remaining sausagemeat.
5 Brush pastry margin with water and position remaining pastry over the sausagemeat so that the edges meet. Press well together.
6 Brush pastry with egg or milk and make four slashes along the top with careless abandon.
7 Cook at 425° or Mark 7 for 15 minutes, then reduce to 350° or Mark 4 for a further 20–25 minutes until golden brown and cooked through.
   Serve hot or cold with vegetables or salad.

SAUSAGE TWISTS

Serves 4   Cooking time 15 minutes

YOU NEED:
1 lb sausages
1 large packet frozen puff pastry
1 beaten egg
Sweet pickle, mustard – or whatever you fancy

METHOD:
1 Grill and cool the sausages.
2 Roll out the pastry very thinly and cut out 4″ × 4″ squares.
3 Divide each one into two triangles and spread with sweet pickle, mustard or what you will!
4 Place a sausage on each one and fold up the pastry – corner to corner.
5 Seal and glaze with the beaten egg.
6 Bake at 450° or Mark 8 for about 10–15 minutes until firm and brown.

This is a splendid warmer. It used to be cooked over a peat fire on a cottage hearth.

DUBLIN CODDLE

Serves 4   Cooking time 1 hour

YOU NEED:
1 lb sausages
¾ lb quartered onions
1 lb quartered potatoes
¾ pint milk

METHOD:
This is one of the few times you prick the sausages, then simply put all the ingredients together with seasoning and simmer gently until the potatoes start breaking up. This will take about an hour or so. It will form a thick, creamy "stew" – and it's ready! It's delicious – especially garnished with parsley and served with fresh greens.

Ever thought of a casserole made from sausages? Vary the vegetables according to what is in season.

CABBAGE &
SAUSAGE CASSEROLE

Serves 4–6   **Cooking time 2 hours**

YOU NEED:
1 lb chipolata sausages
½ lb pickled belly of pork
1 cabbage
1 lb sliced carrots
1 lb sliced potatoes
8 oz sliced onions
8 oz sliced leeks
2 sticks chopped celery
1 cup broad beans
1 cup peas

METHOD:
1 Chop and cook the cabbage in boiling, salted water for 5 minutes and then drain. Do the same with the cut-up pork and throw away the water.
2 Put all the vegetables, except the cabbage, beans and peas, with the pork in the saucepan with 2 quarts of water.
3 Simmer for about 90 minutes (skimming it from time to time).
4 Add the cabbage to the "stew" and now is the moment to add the pricked sausages and put in the peas and beans too.
5 You will need pepper, but the pork usually makes salt unnecessary.
6 Simmer for another 20–30 minutes.

SAUSAGEMEAT ROLL

Serves 4   Cooking time 45 minutes

YOU NEED:
1 lb sausagemeat
2 tablespoons tomato ketchup
1 finely-sliced onion
4 oz grated carrots
2 oz fresh brown breadcrumbs
1 peeled, cored and grated Bramley's Seedling apple
½ teaspoon English mustard powder
2 tablespoons vinegar
2 tablespoons sugar (demerara is ideal)

METHOD:
1 Mix the sausagemeat, ketchup, onion and some seasoning together.
2 Turn this mixture into a greased loaf tin (or ovenproof dish), spreading the mixture evenly so it is not lumpy.
3 Mix the breadcrumbs, apple and carrots together and turn these into the tin just as evenly.
4 Mix vinegar, sugar and mustard and sprinkle over the top.
5 Bake in oven 350° or Mark 4 for 40 minutes.
6 Pour off any excess fat and leave to stand for a few minutes before cutting into slices and serving.
   You can, of course, serve this cold.

This is an extra tasty version of the popular Toad-in-the-Hole. For really crispy batter use a metal dish, not earthenware.

SAUSAGES IN BAKED CHEESEY BATTER

Serves 4   Cooking time 45 minutes

YOU NEED:
1 lb sausages
3 oz flour
1 level teaspoon salt
2 eggs
$\frac{1}{2}$–1 teaspoon made mustard
$\frac{1}{2}$ pint milk
4 oz grated cheese

METHOD:
1 Gradually mix the flour, salt, eggs and mustard into a smooth batter with a wooden spoon.
2 Add the milk a little at a time, beating well; then let it rest, while you grill or fry the sausages until lightly brown.
3 Grease a large tin and heat in the oven at 425° or Mark 7 for 10 minutes.
4 Turn your attention to the batter again and whisk until bubbly.
5 Stir in half the cheese.
6 Mix well and pour in sufficient batter to half fill the tin.
7 Place the sausages in the centre and scatter the remaining cheese over the top.
8 Bake in top of oven for 30 minutes or until well risen and golden brown.
   A skewer or fork inserted in the batter will come out clean when it is cooked.
   Serve immediately, accompanied with salad or buttered green vegetables.

The easy way to make this dish is with packet pastry. Kids love the end result!

SAVOURY SAUSAGE ROLY-POLY

Serves 4   **Cooking time 45 minutes**

YOU NEED:
8 oz sausagemeat
1 medium chopped Bramley apple
1 small chopped onion
2 dessertspoons chopped parsley
Packet of suet pastry
1 beaten egg

METHOD:
1 Mix the apple, the sausagemeat, the onion and parsley well together.
2 Roll out the suet pastry on a well-floured board into a rectangle 9″ wide and about $\frac{1}{4}$″ thick.
3 Spread the sausage mixture over the dough leaving a 1″ border all round.
4 Damp the border lightly and roll up the dough like a Swiss roll. Seal the ends and the join.
5 Line a 2-lb tin with a long strip of greased greaseproof paper or foil, the width of the base.
6 Place the roll in the tin, join downwards, and make 3 or 4 slits in the top to allow the steam to escape.
7 Bake in a pre-heated oven at 400° or Mark 6 for 20 minutes.
8 Lift the roll out of the tin on to a baking tray. Brush over with beaten egg and return to the oven for a further 20 minutes until golden brown.
　　Serve hot with onion gravy and vegetables.

OFFAL

Offal is back in fashion!

Even in four-star restaurants the news that "economy-is-chic" means a return to the table of some long absent dishes.

Cheaper meats in casserole form take longer, slower cooking – but they are just as nutritious as expensive cuts. Here are some tips to help you get the best value.

- Use offal as soon after purchase as possible.
- Kidneys and liver from a pig, and liver from an ox are usually cheaper than the same things from a lamb.
- And if you dip the pig or ox liver in milk for about half an hour before drying and cooking – it will be tastier.
- Make sure the kidneys are skinned, halved and cored before use every time.

Let's start with what the posh restaurants call Tripe a la Caen, and we call:

TRIPE CASSEROLE

Serves 6   Cooking time 6–7 hours

YOU NEED:
3 lb dressed tripe
2 pig's trotters, chopped through
4 leeks
6 medium onions
2 large sliced carrots
1 small bay leaf
½ teacup parsley sprigs
1 level teaspoon thyme
6 cloves
1 pint dry cider, or stock
Seasoning

METHOD:
1 Cut the well-washed tripe into squares and put into a large flameproof casserole dish with the trotters.
2 Slice leeks, onions and carrots and add to the casserole with all the remaining ingredients. If you've got the herbs we mention – now's the time to throw them in.
3 Cover the casserole firmly and cook in the oven at only 275° or Mark 1 for 6–7 hours (ideally when you are using the oven for another dish too, so you don't waste power!)
4 Remove from the oven and keep cold overnight – preferably in the fridge. The next day remove the layer of fat on top.
5 Bring the casserole slowly to the boil on top of the stove and boil for 15 minutes. (If your casserole dish isn't flameproof, just transfer the contents to an ordinary saucepan.)
6 Take out the bones – and bayleaf – before serving.
Goes well with plain boiled potatoes.

Another tasty tripe dish is this one – and it takes less time to prepare.

TRIPE & TOMATO STEW

Serves 4   Cooking time 2½ hours

YOU NEED:
2 lb washed tripe
1 pint each milk and water
6–8 tablespoons oil
2 sliced onions
1 lb chopped tomatoes
¼ lb small mushrooms
1 bay leaf
¼ teaspoon garlic salt
1 tablespoon chopped parsley
Pinch dried rosemary
Pinch nutmeg
¾ pint stock (use cubes)
Seasoning

METHOD:
1 Put the tripe in a large saucepan with the milk and water, add 1 teaspoon salt and bring to the boil. Simmer steadily for an hour.
2 Drain, cool and cut the tripe into strips.
3 Fry onions till soft in hot oil in another pan, then add the mushrooms and the tripe and fry for 2 to 3 minutes.
4 Add tomatoes, herbs and spices (if you have them) and a ½ pint stock.
5 Season, cover and simmer very gently for up to 90 minutes, the tripe should be very tender.
6 Add a little more stock from time to time if stew becomes too dry.
   Serve with creamed potatoes.

Ox hearts are very tasty, and handsomely repay a little time in the cooking. Here are two recipes.

BRAISED OX HEART

Serves 4   **Cooking time 2 hours**

YOU NEED:
1½ lb thinly-sliced ox heart
1 oz seasoned flour
4 oz sliced mushrooms
1 chopped onion
½ lb sliced carrots
2 oz dripping
¼ pint stock

METHOD:
1 Coat the heart slices in seasoned flour and brown in hot dripping before placing in a fireproof dish.
2 Toss the vegetables in the remaining fat and stir in the rest of the flour.
3 Now add the stock and when boiling pour over hearts.
4 Braise in the oven at 325° or Mark 3 for 2 hours.
   Serve with boiled new potatoes or mashed parsnips.

This recipe takes a bit more effort, but it is *so* good!

OX HEART WITH CREAM

Serves 4-6   Cooking time 1½ hours

YOU NEED:
2 lb ox heart
1 large onion
1 leek
2 celery stalks
2 carrots
Seasoning
1½ oz dripping
1½ oz cornflour
2 teaspoons brown sugar
1-3 tablespoons vinegar
2 tablespoons tinned cream (or evaporated milk)
2 cloves and 2 bay leaves (optional)

METHOD:
1 Bring the heart to the boil in a saucepan of cold water.
2 Remove scum and add the onion, sliced vegetables and also add the cloves and bay leaves if you are using them.
3 Season and simmer slowly for about 90 minutes.
4 Take the heart from the pan when it is tender, cool it and slice thinly.
5 Strain the liquor left and save ¾ pint of it.
6 Melt the dripping in another pan – stir in the cornflour and cook for 2-3 minutes.
7 Now add that saved liquor, gradually, and bring to the boil, still stirring.
8 Add the sugar and vinegar to taste.
9 Pop the slices back in the pan and reheat for about 10 minutes.
10 Now stir in the cream or evaporated milk – and serve with potatoes or pasta.

Let's look at what we can do with liver.

LIVER & ONION PIE

Serves 4   **Cooking time 45 minutes**

YOU NEED:
12 oz thinly sliced liver
2 medium, thinly-sliced onions
6 oz sliced mushrooms
2 oz dripping
1¼ lb creamed potatoes (you could use a packet)
1 oz butter
Seasoning

METHOD:
1 Cook the liver in the dripping for about 30 seconds to seal the meat.
2 Remove from the pan and turn the onions and the mushrooms in the dripping for a few minutes.
3 Season well.
4 Place half the liver slices in a greased ovenproof dish, add the onions and then the mushrooms.
5 Put the remaining liver slices on top and cover neatly with the creamed potato.
6 Dot the surface with butter.
7 Bake in oven at 375° or Mark 5 for 45 minutes.

LIVER IN BATTER

Serves 3   **Cooking time 15 minutes**

YOU NEED:
½ lb sliced pig's liver
2 tablespoons flour
Seasoning
½ cup cold water

METHOD:
1 Make a thinnish batter with the last 3 ingredients and dip the slices of liver in – after soaking it in milk for about an hour.
2 Fry in hot oil till golden – and serve with green vegetables.

This is a new way to serve liver. It tastes good and it looks interesting on the plate too!

LIVER ROLLS WITH APPLE

Serves 4   Cooking time 50 minutes

YOU NEED:
8 very thin slices pig's liver
2 oz fresh breadcrumbs
3 medium, finely-chopped onions
1 cored and finely-chopped Bramley Seedling apple
Seasoning
$\frac{1}{2}$ level teaspoon mixed spice
$\frac{1}{2}$ teaspoon grated lemon rind
2 oz butter
1 tablespoon cooking oil
1 level tablespoon flour
$\frac{1}{2}$ pint stock

METHOD:
1 Combine the breadcrumbs, onions, apple, seasoning, spice and lemon rind with 1 oz melted butter.
2 Divide into 8 neat portions.
3 Roll a slice of liver around each portion to enclose, and secure with wooden cocktail sticks (or wrap around with cotton).
4 Heat the remaining oz of butter and the oil in a pan.
5 Brown liver rolls all over and transfer to an ovenproof dish.
6 Stir flour into pan drippings, then add stock and bring to the boil.
7 Season and pour over liver.
8 Cover and cook 325° or Mark 3 for about 50 minutes.
   Serve with a green vegetable.

You can use cooking apples with kidneys too - and make an unusual dish.

KIDNEYS WITH APPLES

Serves 4   **Cooking time 1 hour**

YOU NEED:
1 lb sliced pig's kidneys
1½ oz flour
½ lb sliced onions
1¼ oz butter
1 lb sliced Bramley's Seedling cooking apples
Seasoning
½ pint beef stock (use a cube)
1 bay leaf
½ teaspoon coriander seeds (if you have them)

METHOD:
1 Toss the kidney slices in flour, fry them with the onion in the butter until lightly browned.
2 Transfer to an ovenproof dish, season well, add the bay leaf, coriander and hot stock.
3 Cover with the apple slices.
4 Put a tight-fitting lid on the casserole and cook in the centre of the oven at 325° or Mark 3 for 1 hour.
  If you used a bay leaf, remove before serving.
  Good with boiled potatoes.

Here's a substantial dish which will cheer up the family on a cold day.

KIDNEY PAPRIKA

Serves 4   **Cooking time 30 minutes**

YOU NEED:
1 lb chopped pig's kidneys
$1\frac{1}{2}$ oz butter
1 oz plain flour
1 teaspoon paprika pepper
2 medium chopped onions
8 oz finely-diced carrots
4 chopped tomatoes
$\frac{1}{2}$ pint stock
Seasoning
2 slices bread, toasted and cut into triangles
1 tablespoon chopped parsley

METHOD:
1 Fry onions and carrots in the butter.
2 Toss kidneys in flour and add to pan. Fry gently until they have browned on all sides.
3 Stir in paprika, tomatoes, stock, salt and pepper.
4 Bring to the boil, cover and simmer for 20–25 minutes or until kidneys and vegetables are tender.
 Serve garnished with triangles of toast and sprinkled with parsley to make it look attractive!

A simple dish this – ideal for supper.

KIDNEY-STUFFED BAKED POTATO

Serves 1   Cooking time 2 hours

YOU NEED:
1 large, scrubbed potato
1 kidney   ⎫
1 rasher of bacon ⎬ per person
Seasoning   ⎭

METHOD:
1 Bake the potato for about an hour at 400° or Mark 6.
2 Cut off the top third and hollow out the remainder.
3 Fill it with the kidney which has been wrapped in the rasher of bacon and top up with the potato.
4 Season well, replace top neatly – tying if necessary.
5 Wrap in foil and bake another hour.

Oxtail stew is a super tasty dish – but a lot of people imagine it is very laborious to prepare. Not true! Here's a simplified version cooked on the top of the stove which is cheaper to use than the oven.

But if you are using the oven for something else, you can pop this in too.

SIMPLE BRAISED OXTAIL

Serves 4   Cooking time 3¾ hours

YOU NEED:
1 chopped-up oxtail
2 oz flour
2 oz dripping
1 carrot
1 onion
1 stick of celery
Bunch of herbs
1½ pints stock or water
1 tablespoon lemon juice (or sherry)
Seasoning

METHOD:
1 Trim as much fat as you can from the oxtail pieces, put them in a saucepan of cold water and bring to the boil.
2 Simmer for 15 minutes, then drain and rinse well.
3 Coat the oxtail in flour and fry in a good-sized pan in dripping until each piece is nice and brown all over.
4 Add all the sliced vegetables, the herbs and the stock. Season to taste.
5 Cover the pan firmly and cook gently for at least 3 hours. It's cooked when it's tender.
6 When it is, take it out and keep it warm while you reduce the sauce that's left, by boiling it rapidly.
7 Add the lemon juice (or sherry if you've some to spare).
8 Pour the sauce over the oxtail and serve – plain potatoes make a good accompaniment.

This dish will be even better if you leave it for a day in a cool place before reheating well.

A little stuffing makes a small sheep's heart go much further.

STUFFED SHEEP'S HEARTS

Serves 4–5   Cooking time 2 hours

YOU NEED:
2 sheep's hearts
Little stock

STUFFING:
1 small chopped onion
1 chopped rasher of bacon
4 tablespoons breadcrumbs
1 tablespoon chopped suet
1 teaspoon chopped parsley
Grated rind $\frac{1}{2}$ lemon
1 beaten egg

METHOD:
1 After washing the hearts, cut away the veins and gristle and prepare the stuffing.
2 Just sauté the onion and bacon for a minute or two, then add the rest of the ingredients and bind everything together with the beaten egg.
3 Push the stuffing into the hearts and sew up.
4 Put them in a baking tin with a little stock and bake for about 2 hours, basting often, in a moderate oven 325° or Mark 3.
   Serve with gravy and redcurrant jelly.

FISH

Fish used to be a really cheap alternative to a meat meal, but that's hardly true any longer!

However, there are still some less expensive species which can be used to provide economical dishes. You can buy coley cheaper than cod, for instance, and used in pies and casseroles it is very good indeed – so is pollock and huss, which used to be called Rock Salmon.

Don't ignore these unfamiliar species of fish because they are new. They are also cheaper.

Other cheaper fish include whiting, herring, kipper, mackerel and smoked fish – the latter because it has a stronger flavour and you need less in many recipes.

You can "stretch" fish in various ways – don't just think of it as something to fry or grill. The recipes that follow will give you some ideas.

In many recipes which specify cod or haddock, you can substitute coley or one of the other varieties.

Remember these "new" fish are still a good source of protein, and have a very palatable taste.

To save cash, it's useful to know how much to buy. Here's a guide:

Whole fish   – 8–12 oz per person
Fillets   – 4–5 oz   ,,   ,,
Steaks/Cutlets – 6 oz   ,,   ,,

And here's what to look for when buying fish.

- Eyes should be bright and full, not sunken.
- It should smell fresh and pleasant.
- Fish should be firm not flabby.
- Avoid any watery or fibrous look when choosing steaks or fillets.
- It should have firm, elastic flesh, with bright gills and scales.
- When selecting flat fish, look on the dark side – this shows staleness first. The spots on a fresh plaice, for example, are brightly coloured, but turn brown when stale.
- A fresh herring has bright silver scales and fins and is red round the eyes. Fresh mackerel is even more brightly coloured. Both fish lose their colouring when stale.

Frozen fish should be still frozen hard when bought, and kept in the freezer or ice compartment of the fridge until needed.

Fillets may be cooked from frozen, but never re-freeze frozen fish once it has thawed.

This dish was originally made with cod, but we've substituted coley. Incidentally, it also uses up a "waste" bit of the fish for stock. Use the same method whenever a recipe demands fish "stock" or use the bones and skin from a filleted fish, varying the amount of water to the quantity, i.e. from about 2 pints.

FISH SOUP

Serves 6   **Cooking time 25 minutes**

YOU NEED:
12 oz coley (skinned and cut into small pieces)
2 oz butter
1 large onion
3 sticks of celery
$\frac{1}{4}$ pint of milk
Pinch of saffron (optional)
Generous tablespoon chopped parsley
Seasoning

STOCK:
Make from 2 pints of water and a cod's (or hake's) head. Just drop the fish head in the water and simmer for 25 minutes. Throw the head away and keep the remaining stock.

METHOD:
1 Gently fry the chopped vegetables in the butter in a good-sized pan until they soften.
2 Add the stock, the saffron and seasoning and simmer for 10 minutes.
3 Stir in the milk and parsley and pop in the fish.
4 Simmer for a further 5–10 minutes and it's ready to serve.
   Follow it with an apple and some cheese, and it's a very adequate meal.

Fish

You can also use coley or pollock for fish cakes – which will be a lot cheaper than buying them "ready-made". I assure you the fish content will be higher too!

SIMPLE FISH CAKES

Makes 12–14   **Cooking time 15 minutes**

YOU NEED:
¾ lb cooked fish
1 lb mashed potatoes (you could use a packet)
1–2 teaspoons of chopped parsley (optional but nice)
1 egg (separated)
8 tablespoons of toasted breadcrumbs

METHOD:
1 Mix the fish and potatoes together thoroughly, and add the parsley, egg yolk and some seasoning.
2 Turn out on to a floured board (so it won't stick) and shape into a "Swiss roll".
3 Slice into cakes – about 2 oz each.
4 Coat lightly with the egg white you have left – toss in the breadcrumbs, and fry.

Ever thought of making fish cakes from kippers? Very easy indeed.

KIPPER CAKES

Serves 4   Cooking time 15 minutes

YOU NEED:
½ lb cooked kipper fillets
½ lb mashed potato
1 oz butter
1 beaten egg
1 tablespoon chopped parsley

TO FRY:
1 beaten egg
2 tablespoons breadcrumbs

METHOD:
1 Mix the flaked fish with all the other ingredients and some pepper.
2 Divide into 6–8 cakes about 1″ thick.
3 Dip into the other beaten egg, then the breadcrumbs and fry.
Easy!

Fish

Huss is a firm, meaty fish – ideal for grilling, frying or casseroling.

FRIED HUSS
WITH MOCK HOLLANDAISE

Serves 3–4   Cooking time 15 minutes

YOU NEED:
1 lb Huss
4 oz butter

METHOD:
Cut the fish into 3" pieces and fry in melted butter – as simple
as that!

MOCK HOLLANDAISE:
2 egg yolks
2 tablespoons evaporated milk
$\frac{1}{2}$ pint white sauce
a little lemon (or vinegar)

METHOD:
1 Beat the eggs and evaporated milk together and fold into the
warm white sauce.
2 Heat gently – but don't boil.
3 Add the lemon to "sharpen" the flavour to your own taste and
serve warm with the hot fish.

Skate has a delicate flavour and here's a simple way to use it.

SKATE WITH BLACK BUTTER

Serves 1   Cooking time 25 minutes

YOU NEED:
1 8-oz (or so) "wing" of skate per person

METHOD:
1 Scrape away the jelly-like skin carefully with a very sharp knife.
2 Dot each wing with butter and wrap in foil.
3 Bake for 20–25 minutes at 350° or Mark 4.

BLACK BUTTER:
1 Melt 2 oz of butter in a pan until brown (not "black" despite the name!) and pour over the skate.
2 Immediately put about 1 tablespoon of lemon juice and a pinch of salt into the hot pan until it foams, and pour that over the fish too.
   A few capers, a little parsley – or a sliced gherkin go very well with this.

A pie makes any cheap filleted fish go a long way with little effort.

WHITE FISH PIE

Serves 4–5   **Cooking time 30 minutes**

YOU NEED:
1 lb fillets of any white fish
1 oz flour
1 oz butter
6 oz grated cheese (Cheddar's good)
1 lb mashed potatoes
$\frac{1}{4}$ pint evaporated milk (use the top of the milk in an
  emergency)

METHOD:
1 Poach the fish in seasoned water for about 15 minutes – until
it is nice and tender.
2 Make the $\frac{1}{4}$ pint evaporated milk up to $\frac{1}{2}$ pint with some of the
fish stock you now have, and whisk in the flour.
3 Put the sauce in a pan with the butter and stir it gently over
a moderate heat until it thickens nicely.
4 Take it off the heat and add about 4 oz of the grated cheese
and beat the whole lot until the cheese melts.
5 Drain the fish of the remainder of the stock and flake into a
2-pint dish.
6 Pour on the sauce and mix well.
7 Now pile the potato mash on top and sprinkle on that bit of
cheese you have left.
8 You can place it under the grill to brown – or pop into a hot
oven (if it's already in use) for about 10 minutes.
    A green vegetable goes well with this.

Here are two ideas for casseroling fish. First:

CROFTER CASSEROLE

Serves 4   Cooking time 1 hour

YOU NEED:
4 large cleaned and boned herrings
2 large onions
4 thinly-sliced potatoes
2 oz butter
Seasoning

METHOD:
1 Put the herrings in a greased ovenproof dish, cover with a layer of sliced onions and then a layer of potato slices.
2 Season and dot with butter – and then do the "layering" again.
3 Season and dot with butter again.
4 Cover the dish and bake for 50 minutes in the centre of the oven at 425° or Mark 7.
5 Take the cover off and bake a further 10 minutes to brown the top potatoes.

FISH CASSEROLE

Serves 4   Cooking time 45 minutes

YOU NEED:
1 lb coley or any other white fish
1 lb sliced potatoes
4 oz butter
8 oz sliced onions
8 oz sliced carrots
8 oz sliced mushrooms
2 tablespoons chopped parsley
1 pint fish stock (or water if you must)

METHOD:
1 Boil the potato slices in salted water for about 3 minutes, then drain and line the bottom of an ovenproof dish with them.
2 Cut the fish into 4 and fry it for no more than 30 seconds a side in hot butter.
3 Now take it out and fry the onions and carrots in the remaining butter for a few minutes.
4 Scoop them out and on to the potatoes.
5 Put the fish on top and then toss the sliced mushrooms and parsley into the grease left in the frying pan for 1 minute before scattering this on top of the fish.
6 Pour fish stock over the lot, cover and cook in the centre of a hot oven at 375° or Mark 5 for about 45 minutes.

Herrings are a strong-flavoured fish men usually like. Try:

MUSTARD HERRINGS

Serves 4   Cooking time 30 minutes

YOU NEED:
4 split and boned herrings
3 oz butter
1 teaspoon dry mustard
4 halved tomatoes

METHOD:
1 Open the herrings out flat.
2 Cream the butter, mustard and some seasoning together and spread on each fish.
3 Fold up each fish and wrap each one separately in foil.
4 Bake, with the tomatoes alongside, in the centre of the oven at 375° or Mark 5 for 25–30 minutes.
    You will, of course, remove the foil before serving!

You can use mustard with whiting to cheer up the flavour too. Like this:

WHITING WITH MUSTARD SAUCE

Serves 4   **Cooking time 35 minutes**

YOU NEED:
4 whiting
2 small finely chopped onions
1 tablespoon French, German or even English made mustard
4 tablespoons of stock, water, cider, or white wine if it's your birthday!
Juice of $\frac{1}{2}$ lemon
1 oz butter
1 tablespoon chopped parsley

METHOD:
1 Put the fish in a greased ovenproof dish, season well and scatter finely-chopped onion on top.
2 Blend together the mustard and water (unless you really do happen to have 4 tablespoons of white wine left in a bottle somewhere) and pour over the fish.
3 Cover and bake in the centre of the oven for 20–30 minutes at 350° or Mark 4.
4 Drain the cooking liquor into a handy pan and stir in the lemon juice.
5 Cook for 2–3 minutes to "reduce" before adding the butter and parsley.
6 Pour the sauce over the fish to serve.
   Thin carrots or French beans would make a good accompaniment.

We can't ignore kippers – and this is an unusual way to serve them. Rich people do this with smoked salmon!

KIPPER SOUFFLÉ

Serves 4   Cooking time 40 minutes

YOU NEED:
2 packets kipper fillets
2 oz butter
2 oz flour
$\frac{1}{2}$ pint milk
4 eggs (separated)

METHOD:
1 Start with an oven pre-heated to 375° or Mark 5.
2 Mince the kippers finely.
3 In a pan melt the butter, add the flour and cook gently for a minute.
4 Gradually add the milk (keep stirring all the time as you do) and bring to the boil until it thickens.
5 Stir in the minced kippers and egg yolks and season. Take off the heat.
6 Whisk the egg whites until they are *really* stiff and fold them, a tablespoon at a time, into the kipper mixture. (Don't be too energetic with this job!)
7 Now pour into a greased soufflé dish (about 7") and bake in the centre of the pre-heated oven until risen and firm – about 40 minutes.

Foil is useful in cooking fish – it seals in the flavour. As in this:

MACKEREL BAKE

Serves 4   Cooking time 30 minutes

YOU NEED:
4 cleaned mackerel
1 oz melted butter
1 finely-sliced large onion
4 sliced tomatoes
2 tablespoons chopped parsley

METHOD:
1 Place each mackerel on a piece of foil, cover with a little butter, some sliced onion and a sliced tomato.
2 Sprinkle each with parsley and seasoning and bake at 350° or Mark 4 for 25–30 minutes.
3 Remove from foil and serve with plain boiled potatoes – and a little mustard perhaps!

Another way to use mackerel is with this piquant sauce.

BRETON MACKEREL

Serves 4   Cooking time 20 minutes

YOU NEED:
4 cleaned mackerel
2 egg yolks
2 teaspoons French mustard
2 teaspoons vinegar
1 tablespoon chopped parsley
1 tablespoon chopped chives (you could use onion)
2 oz butter

METHOD:
1 Poach the fish in 1½ pints lightly-salted water with a dash of vinegar for 15–20 minutes until nice and tender. Leave in the water until cool enough to handle.
2 Later lift out carefully. Skin and neatly take out the bones. Place the remaining fillets on dishes and keep warm.
3 Quickly blend together the egg yolks, mustard, vinegar, parsley and chives.
4 Warm the butter to just melt it and add it gradually – until the mixture looks something like mayonnaise.
5 Season and serve over the fillets, accompanied by a green salad and plain new potatoes for perfection.

Fish

Sunday breakfasts in country houses used to offer this dish! We think it's ideal for a Saturday lunch.

KEDGEREE

Serves 5–6   **Cooking time 15 minutes**

YOU NEED:
1 lb smoked fish (haddock is ideal)
4 oz cooked dry rice
2 hard-boiled eggs
2 oz butter
Pinch of cayenne pepper (if it's handy)

METHOD:
1 Poach the fish, remove all skin and bones and flake it with a fork.
2 Cut the white of the eggs into slices and rub the yolks through a fine sieve.
3 Melt butter in a saucepan, add to it the flaked fish, rice, sliced egg-white, pepper and salt, and cayenne to taste.
4 Stir over moderate heat until very hot.
5 Serve on a pre-heated, deep dish, with the yolks sprinkled over it.
   Even nicer with hot toast!

Here's a way of making fish into an exciting meal for children.

BAKED STUFFED POTATOES

Serves 4   Cooking time 1–1½ hours

YOU NEED:
4 large potatoes
½ lb cooked and flaked smoked whiting
7-oz can of sweetcorn
3 oz grated Cheddar cheese

METHOD:
1 Scrub the potatoes clean, prick the skins and bake in a moderate oven 350° or Mark 4 until soft – about 1 hour.
2 With a sharp knife, make a cross that cuts through the skin on top of each potato.
3 Scoop out the cooked centre, mix with the remaining ingredients and season to taste.
4 Pile the mixture back into the potato skins, dot with butter and put into a hot oven 450° or Mark 7 until golden. Serve hot.
   Chopped chives sprinkled over the top add a nice finishing touch if you have them.

The tail end of cod is sometimes cheaper than the rest. You can use it for this.

PARTY-STYLE COD

Serves 4–5   Cooking time 35 minutes

YOU NEED:
2 lb tail end of cod
1 dessertspoon made mustard
$\frac{1}{2}$ oz flour
3 oz melted butter
4 tablespoons cider or white wine
Chopped parsley

METHOD:
1 Spread the skinned fish all over with mustard and place in an ovenproof casserole.
2 Sprinkle with flour and pour on the melted butter.
3 Season and cover, baking in the centre of the oven for about 35 minutes at 375° or Mark 5.
4 Transfer the fish to a warm dish while you tip the cider and parsley into the juices, and boil.
    You can pour this sauce over the fish or serve separately.

EGGS, CHEESE AND VEGETABLES

Meals made from eggs, cheese or vegetables can be just as tasty and nutritious as dishes which use fish and meat.

To keep costs as low as possible choose vegetables in season. The chart tells you which vegetables are normally the 'best buy" – although others will also be available, of course.

When buying eggs, remember there is *no* difference in food value or taste between brown and white eggs – but white are almost always cheaper.

Eggs are high standard protein – and a new safeguard for the shopper means packing dates must be on every pack sold. A figure "1" means eggs were packed during the first week in January – "52" means last week of December.

British eggs (normally the freshest) always bear, in addition, the figure "9".

Store eggs in a cool place (50–55°F) with the pointed end down.

Keep them at room temperature for at least 30 minutes before using.

Cheese is a valuable source of protein, fat and calcium and it does not lose any food value when cooked.

Cheddar is a good all-purpose cheese, and Britain's most popular.

Good cheeses for cooking include Lancashire, Leicester and the Scottish speciality cheeses, Morven and Carrick.

To get the best from vegetables, use them as soon as possible after purchase and don't leave them to soak in water. They lose colour and vitamins.

To cook, put root vegetables (except potatoes) into a saucepan of cold water; green vegetables into boiling water.

As an overall guide to root vegetables, see they are firm with no unsightly blemishes or fibrous roots.

Here is a guide to choosing the best of the most popular vegetables. (Those marked * represent best buys in the season.)

SPRING	SUMMER	AUTUMN	WINTER
Asparagus*	Asparagus*	Aubergines*	Aubergines
Avocado	Aubergines	Avocado	Avocado
pears	Beetroot	Pear	Pears
Beetroot	Broad	Beetroot	Beetroot
Broccoli	Beans*	Broccoli	Broccoli*
Brussel	Cabbages	Brussel	Brussel
Sprouts	Carrots	Sprouts	Sprouts*
Cabbages	Cauliflower*	Cabbages	Cabbages
Celeriac	Chillies	Carrots	Carrots
Chicory	Courgettes	Cauliflower*	Celeriac
Chillies	Cucumber*	Celeriac	Celery*
Courgettes	Florence	Celery*	Chicory*
Florence	Fennel	Chicory	Endives*
Fennel	French	Courgettes	Florence
Home-grown	Beans*	Cucumber*	Fennel
carrots*	Globe	Endives*	Jerusalem
Home-grown	Artichokes	Florence	Artichokes*
Radishes*	Leeks	Fennel	Kale*
Jerusalem	Lettuces*	Jerusalem	Leeks*
Artichokes	Mange-tout	Artichokes	Mushrooms
Kale	Peas	Kale*	Onions
Leeks*	Marrows*	Leeks	Parsnip*
Mushrooms	Mushrooms	Lettuces*	Potatoes
New	New	Marrow*	Salsify
Potatoes	Potatoes*	Mushrooms	Shallots
Onions	Onions	Onions	Spinach
Parsnips	Peas*	Parsnip*	"Spring"
Salsify	Radishes	Peas	Greens
Spinach	Runner	Potatoes	Swedes
Spring	Beans	Runner	Tomatoes
Greens	Salsify	Beans	Watercress
Spring	Spinach	Salsify	
Onions	Spring	Shallots	
Swedes	Onions	Spinach	
Tomatoes	Sweet Corn	Spring	
Turnips	Sweet	Onions	
Watercress	Peppers*	Swedes	
	Tomatoes*	Sweet Corn	
	Watercress	Sweet	
		Peppers*	
		Tomatoes	
		Turnips	
		Watercress	

CHOOSING THE BEST – ROOT VEGETABLES

Jerusalem artichokes
They are pale, warty, ugly looking but have excellent flavour. Avoid any that are too misshapen, small, extra dirty or bruised. Par-boiled they are easier to skin.

Beetroot
Early beets, globe-shaped, are sold in bunches. As they get larger they are sold loose. All roots should be tender, fibre-free, deeply coloured. Over-large samples tend to be coarse.

Carrots
Two types – young spring carrots with foliage sold in bunches and maincrop, cropped and sold loose. Carrots should be well shaped, bright with smooth skins and look "alive". Bunched samples should be about the thickness of a man's thumb with no green in the crowns; maincrop tender with no woody core, washed or unwashed.

Leeks
They should be fresh looking, white, with well-trimmed and no yellow or discoloured leaves.

Onions and shallots
Bulb onions should be firm with feathery skins.

Parsnips
They should have no "fangs" or blemishes. Usually improved by frost, parsnips should always look fresh and have no soft brown patches. Can be bought ready-washed or with dirt on them. The latter tend to keep better.

Potatoes
Home-grown new potatoes start in May. Buy little and often, keep in a cool, dark place, and never peel them – scrub them. With maincrop, the red varieties are best for roasting and mashing, whites for boiling and chipping. Others should be firm and blemish-free.

Swedes
(Yellow or white)
Often unwashed and they should be free of side roots.

Turnips
Fresh, green-foliaged early turnips are sold in bunches, ready washed, and maincrop. Early samples should look good enough to eat raw. With maincrop check for worm holes, sponginess or soft brown patches.

CHOOSING THE BEST – GREEN VEGETABLES

Sprouting broccoli
The shoots should be young, fresh and should snap easily. There are two types – white and purple. The latter is the most widely grown.

Brussel sprouts
No matter what their shade they should be clean, hard, sound, with no yellow leaves. The very tight, small samples often known as *choux de Bruxelles*, although more expensive are less wasteful.

Spring cabbage and greens
Spring cabbage and spring greens should be bright and crisp looking. They need only the minimum of cooking.

Summer and autumn cabbages
They should be firm and solid and of a fresh appearance. The base of the stalk is a good checking point. See that it is clean not slimy. Don't buy if outer leaves have obvious "insect holes".

Winter cabbage
The dark, tough, outer leaves need never be thrown away. Wash them, chop them up and add them to a stock pot or stew. The hearts should be firm and the leaves healthy looking and bright.

White cabbage
Should be round and solid.

Cauliflowers
Avoid badly blown, woolly or badly damaged heads. The base of the stalks should be clean and white. The heads should not be fully developed. Sometimes they can turn a yellowish shade. This does not spoil the taste and these samples are often cheaper.

Kale
Should be fresh, firm, undamaged and without decayed or yellow leaves.

Savoys
Unlike other types of cabbage, a savoy will keep for about a week. The heads are hard, dark-green with crimped, puckered or even blistered-looking outer leaves, and they are big.

Spinach
See it is clean and free from dead, yellow or damaged leaves, flowering shoots and hard stalks. When cooking spinach use only the water already clinging to the leaves after it has been thoroughly washed.

Let's start with something good – and filling.

PLAIN VEGETABLE PIE

Serves 4–6   Cooking time 35 minutes

YOU NEED:
2 diced carrots ⎫
1 small cubed swede ⎪
1 small cubed turnip ⎬ – all cooked
4 oz haricot beans ⎭
1 sliced onion
1 oz fat
2 tablespoons long-grain rice
½ pint parsley sauce (from a packet)
1 tablespoon tomato ketchup
6 oz short pastry (just as cheap to buy it)

METHOD:
1 Fry the onion in the fat for a minute and boil the rice for 10 minutes in salted water, strain and rinse in cold water.
2 Mix these together with the vegetables, parsley sauce and the tomato ketchup.
3 Place the lot in a pie dish and cover neatly with the shortcrust pastry.
4 Bake in a hot oven 400° or Mark 6 for 20–25 minutes until the pastry is a cheerful, golden brown.
   Serve with a jacket potato – and don't count the calories!

Ever thought of using turnips to make a main meal?

TURNIP TOPPERS

Serves 4   **Cooking time 10 minutes**

YOU NEED:
8 large white cooked turnips in chunks
2 finely-chopped, hard-boiled eggs
2 oz fresh breadcrumbs
2 oz grated Lancashire cheese
2 oz butter
Parsley (if it's handy)

METHOD:
1 Toss the chunks of turnips in a frying pan with 1 oz melted butter and then put them into a sizeable, warm pie-dish.
2 Fry the breadcrumbs in the remaining oz of butter until a gorgeous gold.
3 Drain and mix with the hard-boiled eggs which you have thoroughly chopped, and the grated cheese.
4 Sprinkle this evenly over the turnips and grill to a crisp and luscious brown.
  Garnish with the parsley before serving if you wish.

Eggs, cheese and vegetables

You can make mushrooms go a long way with the addition of bought
shortcrust pastry.

MUSHROOM FLAN

Serves 4   Cooking time 1 hour

YOU NEED:
6 oz shortcrust pastry (buy it)
2 teaspoons made mustard
10 oz mushrooms
2 eggs
½ pint milk

METHOD:
1 You need a 7″ flan ring for this (worth buying for a whole
range of flans).
2 Roll out the pastry and line the flan ring with it. Then line the
pastry with foil. This stops it collapsing and is the easy, modern
version of "bake blind".
3 Put it in the oven at 425° or Mark 7 for 10 minutes.
4 Take it out and remove the foil.
5 Spread the base with the made mustard.
6 Chop about 8 oz of the mushrooms finely and put them
evenly over the flan.
7 Separate one of the eggs and put the white in a cup where
it's handy.
8 Mix the remaining yolk with the other egg and just under ½
pint milk.
9 Season well and pour over the mushrooms in the flan.
10 Top this lot with the other 2 oz of mushrooms and bake in
the oven for 45–60 minutes at 350° or Mark 4 until the pastry is
properly cooked.

When vegetables are cheap and plentiful, this flan can be served hot or cold.

FARMHOUSE FLAN

Serves 2   Cooking time 30 minutes

YOU NEED:
6 oz shortcrust pastry (buy it)
1 leek
2 sticks celery
$\frac{1}{2}$ small cauliflower
4 oz grated Cheddar cheese
$\frac{1}{4}$ pint milk
2 eggs

METHOD:
1 Line your 7″ flan with rolled-out pastry.
2 Slice the leek and celery and divide the cauliflower into small pieces.
3 Pop them altogether into a pan, cover with salted water and bring to the boil; simmer for a minute or two.
4 Drain, and place on the uncooked pastry in the flan.
5 Cover with the grated cheese.
6 Beat the eggs into the milk and season.
7 Pour this over the vegetables and cook the flan at 400° or Mark 6 for 30 minutes.

This flan is delicious and the pastry does not need to be cooked first.

SPINACH & CHEESE FLAN

Serves 4   Cooking time 30 minutes

YOU NEED:
6 oz shortcrust pastry (buy it)
12 oz cream cheese
2 eggs
$\frac{1}{4}$ pint milk
1 lb cooked and drained spinach
$\frac{1}{2}$ teaspoon nutmeg

METHOD:
1 Line the flan case with the uncooked pastry, and cover with the cheese and then the spinach.
2 Beat the eggs with seasoning, nutmeg and milk and pour on top of the cheese and spinach.
3 Bake for 10 minutes at 425° or Mark 7, and then lower the temperature to 350° or Mark 4 for another 20 minutes. It's cooked when it's set and golden, and you can eat it hot or cold.

This is particularly economical and nutritious.

CHEESE & EGG TASTY

Serves 4   Cooking time 30 minutes

YOU NEED:
1$\frac{1}{2}$ lb of cooked potatoes
4 tablespoons milk
1$\frac{1}{2}$ oz butter
6 oz cheese
4 hard-boiled chopped eggs
1 tablespoon chopped parsley

METHOD:
1 Mash the potatoes with the milk and butter and season well.
2 Stir in 4 oz cheese, the eggs and parsley.
3 Tip into a greased ovenproof dish, sprinkle with the remaining cheese and bake at 400° or Mark 6 for 30 minutes.
    Especially good with simple salads.

This is a good sustaining dish – ideal for a Monday if you've got cooked potatoes left over from Sunday.

COUNTRY EGGS

Serves 4   Cooking time 15 minutes

YOU NEED:
1½ lb cooked potatoes
2 oz grated cheese
1 chopped onion
2 oz chopped mushrooms
¼ lb chopped streaky bacon
3 hard-boiled eggs
1 oz butter
1 beaten egg for coating
3 oz breadcrumbs
½ oz flour

METHOD:
1 Fry the onion, bacon and mushrooms together in the butter until cooked.
2 Meanwhile, mash the potatoes and chop the eggs.
3 Add to the fried mixture with the cheese, season well and make sure everything is well mixed!
4 Remove from the pan and shape into 8 "cakes".
5 Dust with the flour, coat with the beaten egg, toss in the breadcrumbs and fry in shallow fat until golden brown.
   Serve with a green vegetable – or even eat cold for supper!

I like the idea of a vegetable being used as the basis of a main meal.

CUCUMBER TASTIES

Serves 4   Cooking time 20 minutes

YOU NEED:
1 large cucumber
2 oz butter
1 oz flour
$\frac{3}{4}$ pint milk
3 hard-boiled and chopped eggs
2 oz chopped mushrooms
8 rounds of crisp fried bread
1–2 tablespoons grated cheese

METHOD:
1 Peel the cucumber thinly – and cut into eight pieces. Remove the cores.
2 Drop these "tubes" into boiling, salted water for 5 minutes.
3 Melt 1 oz of the butter in another pan and add the flour.
4 Cook for a few minutes without browning.
5 Add the milk and bring to the boil, stirring all the time.
6 Simmer for 4–5 minutes before adding the chopped eggs, and season.
7 In the other oz of butter (and another pan) fry the mushrooms for a few minutes.
8 Put the fried bread on dishes, arrange the cucumber on top – and fill with the mushrooms.
9 Pour that egg sauce on top, sprinkle with grated cheese and grill till lightly brown.

The financial "low point" of the week is often Thursday – so try this when funds are really low!

THURSDAY LAYER PIE

Serves 4   **Cooking time 45 minutes**

YOU NEED:
2 lb mashed potato
1 lb sausagemeat
1 lb onions
½ teaspoon each thyme and sage
Dripping

METHOD:
1 Grease a pie dish with the dripping.
2 Cut the onions into chunks and boil in salted water – to which you have added the thyme and sage – until tender.
3 Drain well.
4 Put a thin layer of potatoes in the bottom of the pie dish, then sausagemeat, then the onions – and continue to layer until the dish is full (or you've run out of ingredients!)
5 Finish with a layer of potatoes.
6 Dot the top with dripping and bake at 350° or Mark 4 for at least 45 minutes.

Using potatoes for a main meal without meat is hardly known in Britain. But it can be done!

POTATO SOUFFLÉ

Serves 4   Cooking time 40 minutes

YOU NEED:
2 lb boiled potatoes
5 oz grated Lancashire cheese
4 eggs separated
1 oz butter
2 tablespoons single cream (or top of the milk)
2 tablespoons chopped chives

METHOD:
1 Mash the potatoes with the egg yolks, butter, most of the cheese and cream – season well and add the chives.
2 Whisk the egg whites until they are really stiff and fold quickly and carefully into the potato mixture with a metal spoon.
3 Turn into a greased soufflé dish and bake in an oven pre-heated to 425° or Mark 7 for 40 minutes.
   Nice if you garnish it with a few chives and a little grated cheese and serve immediately with a crisp salad.

Marrows are a vegetable which can go a long way if stuffed. This is a change from meat stuffing.

VEGETABLE STUFFED MARROW

Serves 4   **Cooking time 1½ hours**

YOU NEED:
1 peeled marrow
1 oz butter
1 chopped onion
¼ lb sliced mushroom
2 teaspoons chopped parsley
4 chopped tomatoes
½ pint white sauce
4 tablespoons fresh breadcrumbs
8 oz grated Cheddar cheese

METHOD:
1 First slice the marrow lengthwise so it is boat-shaped and remove the seeds.
2 Fry the onion and mushrooms in the butter.
3 Remove them from pan and add to the white sauce with the tomatoes, breadcrumbs, parsley and most of the cheese.
4 Stand each marrow boat on a piece of foil.
5 Now fill each boat cavity with the mixture and top with the cheese you have left.
6 Wrap the foil up and around each boat and pleat over.
7 Bake at 350° or Mark 4 for 1½ hours.

If you've a spot of cream around, this is really good – and not expensive.

PARSNIP & MUSHROOM SOUFFLÉ

Serves 4   **Cooking time 20 minutes**

YOU NEED:
1½ lb cooked parsnips
2 oz butter
4 oz sliced mushrooms
2 tablespoons double cream
4 eggs

METHOD:
1 Liquidize (or sieve) the parsnips with 1 oz of melted butter. This makes a delicious purée on its own but you'll need it for the soufflé!
2 In the remaining oz of butter, fry the mushrooms gently.
3 Separate the eggs and add the yolks, with the mushrooms, to the parsnip purée.
4 Beat in the cream and season.
5 Now's the big moment. Whisk egg whites as stiff as you can (in a separate dish, of course) – and fold them into the purée mixture with a metal spoon.
6 Pour into a greased 1½-pint soufflé dish and bake for 20 minutes in an oven already heated to 450° or Mark 8. Eat immediately.

PASTA

Pasta

Pasta is at least 6,000 years old – and it was probably invented by the Chinese!

It is valuable as a meal "stretcher" or accompaniment to a dish, and has about 13% protein. 12 ounces dry weight provide about 1250 calories.

About 40 shapes, sizes and types are readily available in this country – from noodles to spaghetti – from rings to rigatoni – in different lengths and thicknesses.

Pasta is available in shapes like wagon wheels, stars, cocks' combs, sheets or alphabets!

Its big advantages are that it will keep for ages in the store cupboard and can often be used instead of potatoes – and there is absolutely no preparation or waste.

On the following pages there is a selection of pasta ideas – but you can substitute almost any pasta shape for the ones I suggest.

But – please – don't over-cook it! Here's the proper way:

1 Bring plenty of salted water to the boil.
2 Add the pasta *gradually*, making sure the water continues to boil.
3 Reduce heat to slow boiling. Stir occasionally to avoid sticking.
4 Spaghetti is ready in around 10–15 minutes. Macaroni and short cut shapes around 8–12 minutes (look for cooking time on the pack) but the best way to check is to take a little out of the pan – and bite. It should be firm – not too hard, not too soft.
5 Drain through a sieve, or colander. Return to pan and stir in a knob of butter or spoonful of cooking oil.

This colourful Italian dish is a splendid way to make a little meat go further. It can also stretch the remains of a cooked joint.

PASTA MOUSSAKA

Serves 4   Cooking time 40 minutes

YOU NEED:
3 tablespoons oil
1 lb minced beef or lamb
1 sliced medium onion
14-oz tin of tomatoes
1 bay leaf (if possible)
½ pint creamy white sauce (use a packet)
2–3 oz grated cheese
6 oz green or white lasagne
1 green pepper
2 fresh tomatoes
2–3 tablespoons finely-grated cheese

METHOD:
1 Fry the minced meat and onions in 2 tablespoons of the oil until lightly browned.
2 Add the tin of tomatoes and season with salt, pepper, a pinch of sugar and the bay leaf. Cover and simmer gently for 30 minutes.
3 Meanwhile, make the white sauce, stir in the 2–3 oz grated cheese, and set aside.
4 Cook the lasagne in 2 quarts of boiling, well-salted water until tender, drain thoroughly and toss with the remaining spoonful of oil.
5 Remove the bay leaf and pour the mixture into a shallow ovenproof dish. Spread the lasagne on top.
6 Cover with a thin layer of cheese sauce.
7 Slice the green pepper thinly (throwing away the seeds and membrane), slice the tomatoes and arrange alternately over the dish. Coat again with remaining sauce.
8 Sprinkle with the additional cheese and brown in the oven or under the grill.

The Bavarians use frankfurters for this – you can use sausages if you prefer.

MUNCHEN MACARONI

Serves 4   **Cooking time 15-20 minutes**

YOU NEED:
$\frac{1}{2}$ lb elbow macaroni
4 rashers chopped bacon
1 sliced onion
2 sticks of sliced celery
6 dessertspoons water
3 dessertspoons vinegar
1 level teaspoon sugar
1 chopped gherkin
8 small frankfurters

METHOD:
1 Cook the macaroni in 2 quarts of well-salted water until just cooked and drain thoroughly.
2 Meanwhile, lightly fry the bacon and add the onion and celery for a minute or two.
3 Mix together the water, vinegar and sugar, pour into the pan and bring to the boil.
4 Stir in the cooked macaroni and gherkin, season and keep warm.
5 Cook the frankfurters or sausages.
6 Turn the hot macaroni salad on to a warm serving plate and arrange the hot frankfurters or sausages on top.
     You can use the celery leaves for an attractive garnish if you like.

This is ideal for weekend suppers, because it can be prepared in advance and heated when required.

PASTA PIE

Serves 4   Cooking time 10 minutes

YOU NEED:
¾ pint white sauce (use a packet perhaps)
3 oz grated cheese
Mustard
Salt and pepper
6 oz cut noodles
2 halved tomatoes
6–8 mushroom caps
½ lb chipolata sausages

METHOD:
1 Make the white sauce and stir in the cheese.
2 Season well with mustard, salt and pepper.
3 Cook the noodles in 3 pints of well-salted boiling water until they are just tender, drain thoroughly and add these to the sauce too.
4 Pour the mixture into a buttered shallow pie-dish and arrange the halved tomatoes and mushroom caps (black side uppermost looks prettiest) round the inside edge of the dish.
5 Brown in the oven or under the grill.
6 While you are doing that, grill or fry the sausages until nicely browned and arrange on top.

Try this cheap version of a much posher dish.

MACARONI STROGANOFF

Serves 4–5   Cooking time 15 minutes

YOU NEED:
$1\frac{1}{4}$ lb veal or shoulder pork
2 oz butter
4 oz sliced mushrooms
4 oz chopped onion
2 dessertspoons flour
1 small tin ($2\frac{1}{2}$ oz) tomato purée
1 gill soured cream
$\frac{1}{2}$ lb elbow macaroni
1 tablespoon oil or butter

METHOD:
1 Cut the meat into $\frac{1}{2}$"-thick slices.
2 Fry quickly in heated butter until nicely browned and then remove from pan.
3 Fry the sliced mushrooms and chopped onions gently in the juices until they are just turning colour.
4 Remove the pan from heat and add the flour and tomato purée.
5 Cook gently while stirring and season with a little sugar, salt and pepper.
6 Blend in the sour cream (which means, do it slowly!) and add the meat.
7 If necessary, add a little stock or water so that the meat is covered. Simmer gently for 10 minutes or until the meat is tender.
8 Meanwhile, boil the macaroni in 2 quarts of well-salted water for 8–12 minutes (or until just cooked).
9 Drain well and toss with a spoonful of oil or butter.
10 Arrange in a border round the serving dish, spoon the meat and sauce into the centre.

Hot or cold, this makes a savoury special.

THURSDAY FLAN

Serves 4–5   Cooking time 1 hour

YOU NEED:
6 oz vermicelli
½ oz butter
2 sliced onions
4 rashers chopped bacon
1 tablespoon oil
2 beaten eggs, plus a little milk to make ½ pint
4 sliced tomatoes

METHOD:
1 Cook the vermicelli for about 8–10 minutes and drain.
2 Now this is the clever part – butter an ovenproof pie-dish and press the vermicelli around it to form a "lining".
3 Sauté the onions and chopped bacon in the oil until nice and tender and turn them on to the "lining".
4 Beat the eggs and milk together, season and strain over the onions and bacon.
5 Arrange the tomatoes around the edge of the dish. This looks attractive and also cunningly saves the pasta from crisping up as you:
6 Bake for 35–40 minutes at 350° or Mark 4.

Thought of using pasta with fish? This is incredibly simple.

SMOKEY SURPRISE

Serves 4   Cooking time 15-20 minutes

YOU NEED:
2 cups short-cut macaroni
2 fillets any smoked fish
1 tin condensed mushroom soup

METHOD:
1 Poach the fish in a little milk.
2 Cook the macaroni.
3 Flake the fish and add it to the pan with the soup and the macaroni.
4 Heat thoroughly and serve – preferably to applause – with, say, tomatoes and peas.

Everything you need for this dish should be already in your store cupboard. Hence its name.

RAINY DAY PIE

Serves 4–6   Cooking time 40 minutes

YOU NEED:
4 oz macaroni
$15\frac{1}{2}$-oz can minced beef with gravy
2 tablespoons tomato ketchup
2–3 slices bread and butter in triangle shapes

METHOD:
1 Cook and drain the macaroni – return it to the pan and stir in the minced beef, ketchup and seasoning.
2 Turn into a greased, shallow, ovenproof dish and top with the bread, butter side up.
3 Bake for about 30 minutes at 400° or Mark 6 until the bread is crisp and golden.
   Goes well with a green vegetable.

A 7-oz can of the cheapest salmon makes a tasty lunch or supper, extended like this.

SALMON SUPPER

Serves 4   Cooking time 20 minutes

YOU NEED:
6 oz pasta shells
2 chopped hard-boiled eggs
7-oz can salmon
2 oz butter
1 tablespoon chopped parsley

METHOD:
1 Cook the shells and drain.
2 Drain the salmon (save the juice, you are *not* going to waste it!) and flake it.
3 Put the shells back into the pan with the butter, parsley, salmon (and juice) and the eggs.
4 Gently reheat, giving the mixture an occasional stir.
5 Turn into a heated dish and serve.
Goes very well garnished with cucumber.

Cheap, quick – what better for midweek?

MACARONI LYONNAISE

Serves 4   **Cooking time 30 minutes**

YOU NEED:
3 oz butter
½ lb sliced onions
1½ oz flour
¾ pint milk
6 oz macaroni
4 hard-boiled halved eggs
3 oz grated cheese

METHOD:
1 Fry the onion in the butter until softened – stir in the flour, blend in the milk, simmer and season and cook gently for 20 minutes.
2 Meanwhile, cook the macaroni, drain and add to the sauce.
3 Pour half of the mixture into an ovenproof dish, arrange the eggs on top and cover those with the remaining mixture.
4 Sprinkle generously with the grated cheese.
5 Dot with butter and grill until golden brown and bubbling.
   Super with salad.

PUDDINGS

Puddings

We no longer eat the same quantity of steamed puddings, "roly-polys" and the heavier desserts of a generation ago.

The reasons are a mixture of more central heating, figure-consciousness and better general diet.

This leaves us with finding a whole new range of desserts to end our family meals – while keeping some of the old style puds.

Again, for economy, when using fruit – use it in season. For pies and puddings or for stewing about 4–5 oz per person is a good guide.

You can frequently use a sugar-substitute instead of the real thing to save calories – but you won't really save money. Follow the instructions on the bottle or packet to "translate" the substitute into the spoonfuls of ordinary sugar in the recipes. But it won't work in the heavier, baked puddings which require the sugar bulk.

It's a good idea to stretch more expensive fruit with flavoured jellies and moulds.

POOR MAN'S APPLE CHARLOTTE

Serves 6   **Cooking time 45 minutes**

YOU NEED:
2 lb cooking apples
1 lemon
6 oz demarara sugar
4 oz white breadcrumbs
1½ oz melted butter

METHOD:
1 Pre-heat the oven to 375° or Mark 5.
2 Grate the lemon rind and mix with 4 oz of the sugar and the breadcrumbs.
3 Peel, core and slice the apples and toss in the juice from the lemon and the remaining 2 oz of sugar.
4 Layer first the apples, then the breadcrumb mixture in an ovenproof dish – finishing with breadcrumbs.
5 Pour the melted butter on top and bake for about 45 minutes till crunchy and golden on top.

Jelly can make biscuits into a pudding – especially "soft" biscuits which would otherwise be thrown away.

BISCUIT SUNDAE

Serves 4   **Cooking time 5 minutes**

YOU NEED:
1 packet lime jelly
1 small can evaporated milk
4–6 oz chocolate biscuits

METHOD:
1 Make up the jelly with $\frac{3}{4}$ pint of water; cool, and leave until almost set.
2 Use this time to chill and whisk the evaporated milk until really thick.
3 Slowly add the cooled jelly, whisking constantly, until the mixture itself is again really thick.
4 Crunch the chocolate biscuits (a quick way is to put them in a polythene bag and roll with a rolling pin) then layer jelly and chocolate crumbs into tall glasses – also finishing with jelly.
5 Chill and serve.

SIMPLE EGG CUSTARD

Serves 2   **Cooking time 5 - 10 minutes**

YOU NEED:
1 egg
$\frac{1}{2}$ pint milk
Sugar to taste
Grated nutmeg (optional)

METHOD:
1 Whisk the egg and milk together lightly.
2 Add enough sugar to please you, and pour into a saucepan.
3 Put it over the lowest possible heat and stir constantly until it's nice and thick – it must not boil.
4 Pour into 2 dishes, sprinkle the nutmeg on top if you have it – or let it cool and decorate in any way you like.

Here's how to make a few raspberries go much, much further.

RASPBERRY MOUSSE

Serves 4

YOU NEED:
8-oz can of raspberries
Packet of raspberry jelly
Small can evaporated milk

METHOD:
1 Drain the raspberries and dissolve the jelly in the juice in a pan over a very low heat.
2 Sieve the raspberries or put through a blender and add to the jelly mixture.
3 Allow it to cool while you chill the evaporated milk.
4 When cool, whisk the evaporated milk and the cooled jelly together until it is lovely and thick.
5 Pour into a mould or pretty dish and chill till set. Simple!

When gooseberries are plentiful this makes a tempting dessert.

GOOSEBERRY LAYERS

Serves 4–6   Cooking time 5-10 minutes

YOU NEED:
4 oz butter
2 oz soft brown sugar
6 oz fresh breadcrumbs
$1\frac{1}{2}$ lb gooseberries (cooked and drained)

METHOD:
1 Fry the breadcrumbs in the butter and 1 oz of the sugar until crunchy and golden.
2 Leave to cool and stir in the remaining sugar.
3 Beginning and ending with crumbs, layer with the gooseberries into serving dishes.
4 Chill well and serve with cream on Sundays – cold custard the rest of the time!

Pancakes can be eaten any day – not just on that Tuesday! Here's a basic recipe – and a few filler ideas. The oil makes the mixture more "velvet-like" – it isn't strictly necessary.

ANYDAY PANCAKES

Makes 4–6   **Cooking time 8–12 minutes**

YOU NEED:
4 oz flour
1 egg
½ pint milk
1 tablespoon oil
Pinch of salt

METHOD:
1 Add the salt to the sifted flour in a bowl, make a well in the centre and drop in the beaten egg.
2 Add half the milk and beat the liquid with the flour.
3 Whisk away for a minute or two and then whisk in the rest of the milk and the oil. Beat until the mixture is really smooth.
4 You need only 2–3 tablespoons for the average frying pan, nicely oiled and hot.
5 Cook the pancakes for only a minute each side.
   For fillers try these, instead of the eternal lemon juice, sugar or jam: cottage cheese and raisins; stewed apples, or other fruit; syrup or ice cream.

LEMON DELIGHT

Serves 4   Cooking time 2 hours

YOU NEED:
2–4 tablespoons lemon curd
4 oz butter
4 oz caster sugar
Grated rind of a lemon
4 oz self-raising flour
2 eggs
Little milk

METHOD:
1 Butter a $1\frac{1}{2}$–2-pint pudding basin and put 2 tablespoons or so of lemon curd in the base.
2 Cream the butter and sugar together and beat in the eggs.
3 Toss in the lemon rind.
4 Fold in the flour a little at a time and add enough milk to make it "dropping" consistency.
5 Pour this mixture into the basin, cover well with foil and steam for about 2 hours.
6 Turn out and serve with remaining lemon curd heated.

You can use macaroni to make a winter pud.

MACARONI PEACH

Serves 4–5   **Cooking time 50 minutes**

YOU NEED:
3 oz macaroni
1½ oz butter
1½ oz flour
¾ pint milk
2–3 oz caster sugar
2 separated eggs
8-oz can peaches

METHOD:
1 Start by pre-heating the oven to 325° or Mark 3.
2 Cook the macaroni in boiling water for 6 minutes on top of the stove. Drain.
3 Make a sweet white sauce by cooking the butter and flour together for a minute then adding the milk and ½–1 oz sugar. Boil up for a few minutes, stirring all the time.
4 Leave this to cool before you add the beaten-up egg yolks and drained macaroni.
5 Put into a 1-pint ovenproof dish and add the drained peaches.
6 Whip the egg whites until stiff and whisk the remaining sugar in lightly.
7 Pile this on top of the peaches and bake in the centre of the oven for 45 minutes – until brown and firm on top.
   No peaches? Try apricots – or any other similar tinned fruit.

Bread can be used as a base for a number of delicious puddings.

SPECIAL
BREAD & BUTTER PUD

Serves 4–6   **Cooking time 40 minutes**

YOU NEED:
8 slices bread and butter
3 oz jam or marmalade
2 eggs
2 oz sugar
Small can evaporated milk made up to ¾ pint with water

METHOD:
1 Make jam or marmalade sandwiches with 6 of the bread slices.
2 Cut into squares and arrange in layers in a greased pie dish.
3 Beat the eggs with the sugar and the milk mixture, pour over the bread and leave to soak for an hour or so.
4 Cut the remaining 2 slices of bread and butter into triangles, strips or anything else which pleases you and arrange prettily on top – butter side up.
5 Bake for 30–40 minutes at 350° or Mark 4 until the pudding is set and crisp and brown.

FAIRY FINGERS

Serves 3–4

YOU NEED:
6 slices bread and butter
2 oz jam
1 egg
1 small can evaporated milk
1 teaspoon sugar
2 oz cooking fat
Little sugar

METHOD:
1 Make jam sandwiches – trim the crusts and cut into fingers.
2 Beat the egg, milk and sugar together and dip the fingers into this mixture, coating all over.
3 Heat the fat in a pan and fry the fingers till golden.
4 Drain on kitchen paper, sprinkle with sugar and serve to an admiring family.

RED PEARS

Serves 4   Cooking time 20 - 30 minutes

YOU NEED:
4 under-ripe pears
1-lb jar redcurrant jelly
Juice of a lemon
Red food colouring

METHOD:
1 Rinse a saucepan in cold water (it helps to stop it sticking).
2 Melt the jelly in the pan with the lemon juice and a drop or two of colouring.
3 Peel the pears and cook slowly in this syrup for 15–20 minutes – or until soft.
4 Drain the pears and put them into individual dishes.
5 Boil the syrup until reduced to about $\frac{1}{4}$ pint, pour over the pears and serve.

When pears are cheap, try these.

SAUCY PEARS

Serves 4   Cooking time 15 minutes

YOU NEED:
8 oz sugar
1 pint water
4 peeled and cored firm pears
4 tablespoons drinking chocolate
1 teaspoon cornflour
2 tablespoons milk

METHOD:
1 Bring the sugar to the boil in a pan with the water and stir it constantly until it dissolves.
2 Now stand the pears upright in the syrup and simmer over a low heat for 10–12 minutes, after which the pears should be just tender.
3 Drain the syrup (but don't throw it away) and set the pears aside to get cold.
4 When they are, put $\frac{1}{4}$ pint of the syrup back into a pan and boil.
5 Blend the drinking chocolate with the cornflour and milk in a dish and stir into the bubbling, boiling syrup.
6 Cook for about 1 minute, stirring all the time. Leave to become cold.
7 To serve, put the pears into dishes and coat with the cold chocolate sauce.

Home-grown rhubarb is often the cheapest of fruit. Remember it doesn't have to be peeled.

SUNDAY RHUBARB

Serves 6

YOU NEED:
2 lb rhubarb, cut into 2″ pieces
2 egg yolks
Knob of butter
½ pint milk (less two tablespoons)
1 dessertspoon caster sugar
Vanilla flavouring
Grated milk chocolate, nuts or anything else you fancy for
   decoration

METHOD:
1 Poach the rhubarb gently in no more than a tablespoon of water with the butter, until tender; strain off the juice and save 6 pieces of rhubarb. (The butter takes away the acidity which sometimes puts your teeth on edge!)
2 Sweeten the remainder to your liking and then serve or liquidize, and cool.
3 Warm the milk and sugar in a pan and pour over the beaten egg yolks.
4 Now cook this over another pan of boiling water, stirring occasionally, until the mixture thickens to an egg custard.
5 Stir in a little vanilla essence and leave to get cold.
6 When it is, mix the rhubarb purée into the custard – add just a spoonful of rhubarb juice if it's too thick.
7 Pour into 6 of your nicest glasses, pop a rhubarb piece on top with any decoration you have – and serve.

When other fruit is expensive – lemons make good puddings.

UPSIDE-DOWN DELIGHT

Serves 4   Cooking time 45 minutes

YOU NEED:
2 oz butter
3 oz caster sugar
1 lemon
2 eggs separated
2 oz self-raising flour
$\frac{1}{4}$ pint milk

METHOD:
1 Preheat the oven to 350° or Mark 4 while you cream the butter and sugar with the grated lemon rind and all the juice you can squeeze out.
2 Beat in the egg yolks, add the flour and the milk and mix very well.
3 Whisk the egg whites you have left until stiff and fold into the mixture.
4 Pour into a ready-greased 2-pint ovenproof dish and bake in the centre of the oven for 35–45 minutes.
5 Turn out to serve – so the top is a sponge which is floating in the lemon sauce.